Professional Values and Practice

Achieving the Standards for QTS

James Arthur, Jon Davison and
Malcolm Lewis

RoutledgeFalmer
Taylor & Francis Group

LONDON AND NEW YORK

First published 2005
by RoutledgeFalmer
2 Park Square, Milton Park, Abingdon, Oxon OX14 4RN

Simultaneously published in the USA and Canada
by RoutledgeFalmer
270 Madison Avenue, New York, NY 10016

RoutledgeFalmer is an imprint of the Taylor & Francis Group

© 2005 James Arthur, Jon Davison and Malcolm Lewis

Typeset in Sabon by
Integra Software Services Pvt. Ltd, Pondicherry, India
Printed and bound in Great Britain by
TJ International Ltd, Padstow, Cornwall

British Library Cataloguing in Publication Data
A catalogue record for this book is available from the British Library

Library of Congress Cataloging in Publication Data
A catalog record for this book has been requested

ISBN 0–415–31726–6 (hbk)
ISBN 0–415–31727–4 (pbk)

Contents

Introduction

This book is concerned with the values and personal capabilities which are central to professionalism in teaching. It is primarily intended for those on programmes of initial teacher education and training who are working towards Qualified Teacher Status (QTS), and their tutors and mentors, but it is also for all teachers who are committed to developing their professional practice, and is relevant to those who are pursuing one of the Student Associate schemes designed to provide undergraduate students with experience of the teaching profession. Each of the chapters principally addresses one of the eight Standards for Professional Values and Practice in *Qualifying to Teach* (TTA, 2002; revised 2003). We are concerned, however, not just with explicating and discussing the Standards for QTS with the intention of providing guidance to new teachers entering the profession, but with explorations of ethical dimensions of teaching, and personal attributes and dispositions which go well beyond the minimum expectations embodied in the QTS Standards and have a direct bearing on all aspects of professional behaviour.

While the book's principal focus is the Standards for QTS which apply in England and Wales, it is also relevant to those following professional training programmes in other places. Wherever teachers are trained and licensed to teach, attempts have been made to set out the skills, competences, knowledge, understanding, core values and dispositions that are expected of new teachers. Recent years have seen determined drives by governments and their departments of education in all parts of the United Kingdom towards establishing the Standards by which entry into the profession is regulated, and the requirements with which all training courses must comply for recognition and accreditation. In England and Wales, this drive started in earnest in 1992 with the publication of the first set of nationally required 'competences'. What has happened in the UK is paralleled in many other countries and states where control of entry into teaching is formally regulated and licensed. In Northern Ireland it takes the form of the Department of Education Northern Ireland's *Teacher Education Partnership Handbook* setting out the roles and responsibilities of the various teacher education partners. Scotland has its own *Guidelines for Teacher Education Courses in Scotland* published by the Scottish Executive Education Department in 1998, with all courses requiring accreditation by the General Teaching Council of Scotland. In the United States every state has its own teacher licensing requirements, and there are several different organisations competing with each other as agencies which accredit teacher education programmes, each with its own formulation of what constitutes professionalism in teaching.

Six years after the appearance in 1992 of the first competences in England and Wales came a new formulation in 1998 of 'Standards' for QTS, published jointly by the then Department for Education and Employment and the recently established Teacher Training Agency (TTA). This was quickly accompanied by an extremely detailed 'National Curriculum for Initial Teacher Training'. Attempts to specify the content of teacher training in precise detail replicated the worst excesses of the first formulations of the National Curriculum for schools following the 1988 Education Reform Act. It was an unwieldy instrument and was roundly criticised for signally failing to capture many of the fundamental characteristics of good teaching. It did exactly what the Northern Ireland effort set itself *against* doing when saying that, 'The atomisation of professional knowledge, judgement and skill into discrete competences inevitably fails to capture the essence of professional competence.' For all its attempts to be atomistically comprehensive, the 1998 version of the Standards for QTS and the National Curriculum for ITT conspicuously omitted any significant reference to professional values and attitudes and those personal dispositions which most people vividly remember in the teachers who made most impression on them.

By 2002 the message had begun to get through, and the establishment of the General Teaching Council for England (GTCE) (long campaigned for, and more than 35 years after Scotland's example to the UK in establishing its GTC) contributed to putting professional attributes on the agenda of teacher education and training in England and Wales. As a result, the publication in that year of a more streamlined set of Standards for QTS devoted its first section to 'Professional Values and Practice', explicitly referenced to the GTCE Code of Professional Values and Practice for Teachers, formally agreed by the GTCE in February 2002.

We take the view that while the QTS Standards for Professional Values and Practice and the GTCE Code of Practice are welcome developments in the relatively recent history of codifying the professionalisation of teaching, they are not as they stand at present complete or unarguable. They are still expressed in terms which emphasise instrumental practice and knowledge and mask the subtleties and complexities of the personal challenges they involve. We have no wish to propose any more comprehensive formulations, and especially not a return to the prescriptive – and ultimately stultifying – forensic detail represented by earlier formulations. We deeply believe that the more intrusive the attempts of central regulating bodies to define 'the essence of professional competence' are, the less encouragement there is for creative and enlightening discussion and reflection about what that essence comprises. At the heart of our thinking is our desire to give prominence to exactly that discussion and reflection which we regard as central imperatives in mature professionalism. We see what is contained in the QTS Standards as starting points for this discussion and reflection, not simply and merely the hurdles which those qualifying to teach must clear. In this we acknowledge that our disposition towards the Standards is to some extent in opposition to the avowed intention informing them: that they are statements of the 'outcomes' which are expected of teacher education and training programmes. This is, we believe, far too simplistic, and dishonours the real complexities that are involved. Its tendency is to reduce what is often highly problematic in the experience of being or becoming a teacher to those 'discrete competences' which can be conveniently evidenced and then 'assessed' as outcomes. The following view, from the United States as it happens, expresses this tendency well. We want this book to make a contribution to joining things together in practice:

> Although complicated, teaching nonetheless evokes simple, reductionist analysis. Much of the discourse on teaching and learning pulls apart what must be joined in practice.
>
> (National Board for Professional Teaching Standards, 1989)

The same publication goes on to talk about professionalism in teaching, entailing the 'ongoing pursuit of these unities', and how 'teachers regularly find themselves confronting hard choices – sometimes sacrificing one goal for another, sometimes making compromises'.

Nowhere is this more true than in the arena of professional values, and this book is concerned with encouraging its readers to consider the multi-dimensionality of what formulations such as the Standards for QTS present in this respect. True professionalism, we believe, partly consists in possessing the readiness, and the analytical ability, to face dichotomies and dilemmas, and to apply to their consideration an increasingly secure imagination and intelligence which develops from reflection on personal experience and on the analyses of others. This is, essentially, a profoundly *educational* enterprise, and it is why we regularly couple together the words 'education' and 'training' throughout the book, and are not content with the label 'Initial Teacher Training'.

Each chapter addresses a particular Standard, though with some common themes and issues interweaving all of the chapters, and we therefore encourage readers to take the chapters in whatever order they choose. Each chapter includes, either at the end or embedded within it, invitations in the form of tasks or exercises to consider various practical situations or engage in applying understanding to professional experience. These are included not to mimic conventional textbooks' apparent interests in making their student readerships 'do some work' (as if the act of reading were not work enough), but to encourage readers to do just that 'pursuing of unities' and 'joining together in practice' to which reference has been made. The aims of these activities are to prompt reflection and analysis, and to take time out to consider the choices or compromises through which you might resolve – or, rather, work towards finding a satisfactory way of living with – complex, problematic or uncertain situations.

1 Professional Values and Practices in Teaching and Learning

...ethics is relevant to anyone who ever asks the question 'what ought I to do' or 'would this be right?' It is of relevance to anyone who ever makes moral judgements about others, who ever praises or condemns people's actions. It is of particular importance in education because not only are teachers and administrators beset with moral questions, but now, more than ever, they are responsible for the moral well-being and education of their pupils, the future generation.

Haynes, *The Ethical School* (1998: 3)

INTRODUCTION

The discourse of government policy on teacher education and training has been conducted, for the most part, in terms of 'competences', 'standards', 'skills' and 'outcomes'. Officially, very little attention is paid to purpose, to questions of meaning. Almost as little attention has been given to the wider purpose of the Standards to be attained by the student teacher. The emphasis in the new Standards documentation (*Qualifying to Teach: Professional Standards for Qualified Teacher Status and the Requirements of Initial Teacher Training*, TTA: 2003) is still largely on what the teacher can do, rather than what the teacher is and can become: if the sole focus is on the teacher as needing to acquire certain skills, then 'training' is considered only in terms of methods and techniques. Whilst the new Standards have an introductory section on professional values, they remain largely a competence-based model of teacher training. The Standards still portray the teacher as a technician charged with specific tasks that are measurable in outcome. Whilst there is a clear desire to make teaching a more rigorous and more accountable discipline, the above process could undermine teacher professionalism. How does such methodology meet the concept of professional values? This enquiry itself begs two further questions: 'What is a profession?' and 'What do we mean by professional values?'

A profession can be defined by the recognition of the social and moral context of its work. The GTCE believe that an increased awareness of the value dimensions and responsibilities of teaching is essential for both teacher professionalism and for improved practice. To accept a model of the teacher as one who only systematically *transmits* knowledge is to deny the professionalism of the teacher, and to reduce teacher education to the production of skilled technicians. If, on the other hand, we focus on the teacher as professional, we need to address issues about human development and the purpose of education. It is our contention that these issues, far from being marginal, are in fact at the centre of teacher education, and that without them teaching becomes a mechanical skill, incapable of promoting or enhancing the personal, social and moral development which the government professes to favour. It is in this context that student teachers may begin to approach the question of professional values.

The idea that teaching can be narrowly based on producing quantifiable learning outcomes, which, at present, constitute the major criteria of teaching competence, is highly questionable. As you will discover the teacher is not simply one whose contribution is limited to the systematic transmission of knowledge in a school. The demonstration of professional values goes beyond the demonstration of your classroom competence. By concentrating on practical teaching skills and methods – the mechanics of teaching – it is possible to produce a teacher who is able to manage a class and instruct pupils. However, professional teachers are aware of the larger social setting, have the flexibility to anticipate change, to adapt their methods to new demands and when necessary to challenge the requirements laid upon them. To produce such professional teachers we need to strike a balance between a focus on the development of competence and raising the student teachers' awareness of the meaning of their task. This may be achieved by encouraging student teachers to see their daily teaching in the perspective of larger theories of human development and social policy, for it should always be remembered that the teacher is also 'educator' – one who helps form human beings. Good teachers sense the importance of acquiring a wider perspective on human values. Standards must exist within a framework of the personal values and qualities appropriate to the teaching profession. Student teachers need to be encouraged to develop a commitment to professional values that they are able to demonstrate through their personal example. Newly Qualified Teachers require not only Standards or competences, but also professional value commitments.

To gain QTS you need to demonstrate that you have met the Standards published by the government. The new Standards have an opening section on professional values numbered 1.1–1.8 as follows:

1. Professional Values and Practice

Those awarded Qualified Teacher Status must understand and uphold the professional code of the General Teaching Council for England by demonstrating all of the following:

1.1

They have high expectations of all pupils; respect their social, cultural, linguistic, religious and ethnic backgrounds; and are committed to raising their educational achievement.

1.2

They treat pupils consistently, with respect and consideration, and are concerned for their development as learners.

1.3

They demonstrate and promote the positive values, attitudes and behaviour that they expect from their pupils.

1.4

They can communicate sensitively and effectively with parents and carers, recognising their roles in pupils' learning, and their rights, responsibilities and interests in this.

1.5

They can contribute to, and share responsibly in, the corporate life of schools

1.6

They understand the contribution that support staff and other professionals make to teaching and learning.

1.7

They are able to improve their own teaching, by evaluating it, learning from the effective practice of others and from evidence. They are motivated and able to take increasing responsibility for their own professional development.

1.8

They are aware of, and work within, the statutory frameworks relating to teachers' responsibilities.

These professional value Standards have statutory force, but they are generally not explicit about practices and are not framed in terms of ethical values. It is left to teacher education courses to interpret them and this is an opportunity for the teaching profession as well as teacher educators to make these professional values more explicit. Admittedly, the Standards are an improvement on the competence statements of Circular 9/92, but how can student teachers put these 'value Standards' into practice when there is no clear statement of what is expected of them in practice? All that may possibly be achieved in using these professional Standards is to make wider inferences about appropriate behaviour by student teachers. Some would argue that it is not desirable to set Standards in professional values since there can be no real agreement about what they mean in practice. Halstead and Taylor (2000: 177) recognise that two assumptions lie behind the Standards in professional values for teachers. First, that teachers see it as their role to influence the development of their pupils' values. Second, that pupils' values are 'influenced, consciously or otherwise by the example set by their teachers in their relationships, attitudes and teaching styles'.

The Teacher Training Agency (TTA) produced a second edition of *Qualifying to Teach: Handbook of Guidance* in the summer of 2003 that provides a brief commentary on the Standards for teaching. On each of the eight Standards on Professional Values and Practices the document first outlines the scope of the Standard and then proceeds to offer suggestions on how to use the Standards in making judgements about student teachers by detailing the kinds of evidence relevant to meet them. It is most relevant to teacher educators, particularly in performing their 'assessor' role or function. However, as every student teacher soon recognises it is the teacher–pupil relationship that lies at the heart of the practice of education. As Bonnett (1996: 35) says, teaching is about the engagement of the personhood of the teacher with the personhood of the pupil – 'a genuine mutual responsiveness initiated by the teacher's desire to enable authentic learning'. This is why a strong sense of personal identity infuses the work of a good teacher. In addition, the Standards are to be demonstrated without the student having engaged in the theories that underpin professional ethics. Teachers educated in the 1970s and 80s will know from Peters (1965) that teaching is undertaken in ways which accord with such moral principles as those of truth-telling and respect for persons. The new Standards are only a start in attempting to meet the challenges of the teaching profession and should be viewed as part of the student teachers' professional commitment to self-reflective practice.

PROFESSIONALISM

By professional values we mean the complex sets of beliefs that it is considered positive and appropriate for teachers to hold, and the actions by which those beliefs may be communicated to pupils. Values are an integral part of teaching, reflected in what is taught and also in how teachers teach, and interact with, pupils. Pupils spend the greatest amount of their daily time with teachers, who have significant opportunities to influence them. The teacher's role is truly formative for at the heart of the practice of education is the relationship between teacher and pupil. It is this relationship which sets the tone for all else in the classroom. As Kelly (1995: 105) reminds us, 'The provision of education is both a moral and a practical imperative in a democratic society.' The very purpose of schools is to make a difference to the lives of pupils and so the moral and ethical dimensions of teaching provide the core value context in which teachers are located. Values are central to competent professional practice, but competence-based models of teacher training are widely believed to have no commitment to professional values (Hyland, 1993). That is why there is growing interest in defining and assessing ethical judgement and values in the professional education of teachers.

The attempt to encapsulate the full range of human abilities and adaptations within the concept of competence or Standards is simply not possible. As Strain (1995: 47–48) observes:

> Professionality is inextricably bound up with widely shared values, understandings and attitudes regarding the social order and the rules by which others, in certain relationships, may instigate a claim on us…to claim the standing of a professional has come to mean adherence to an ethic, a moral principle, which derives from a freely undertaken commitment to serve others as individual human beings, worthy of respect, care and attention.

Teaching is above all a 'self-giving' enterprise concerned with the good of pupils. Since values are embedded in the Standards by which we assess and help develop student teachers, there is clearly scope for systematic assessment of competent professional practice in teaching within a values context.

At present teacher 'training' may be sliding into a world of totally instrumental purposes in which *explicit* values disappear. The new Teach First programme of teacher education demonstrates this instrumental approach. The official Department for Education and Skills (DfES)/TTA Standards for teaching are not value-free, they are *implicitly* instrumental and that is why their meaning should be clearly displayed and their ramifications explored. The aim of the teacher training Standards model is to realise some predetermined goal which is often treated as unproblematic in discussion and operation. It is clear that if one includes attitudinal or value dimensions in Standards then the criteria of achievement are not so easily identifiable. Bland statements of professional values, which receive general agreement, are rarely associated with tangible outcomes or with actual activities undertaken by teachers in school. The list of government Standards includes some personal attributes which will demand considerable sensitivity in assessment. There is a tendency in education today to turn questions into an objective problem to be solved with a corresponding technical solution. There is an obsession with 'technical' solutions in schools and yet many have become teachers because they once believed that ideas and insight are at least as real and powerful as the world of Standards and Office for Standards in Education (OFSTED) grades.

Nevertheless, we believe it is necessary to allow ideas and suggestions to emerge from within the teaching profession itself. The teaching profession has only begun to generate the teaching principles to which teachers would wish their actions to conform. Against this, the word 'professional' in teaching is increasingly equated with skill and efficiency. The conception of professional values and responsibility in teaching is too narrow when restricted to technological criteria of functional success. Teachers are role models, and it follows that, when, in the classroom, a student teacher exhibits values or personal characteristics which are held to be at variance with what is educationally desirable for pupils to acquire, then there is cause for concern. Part of your task as a student teacher is to recognise, acquire and practise professional values in teaching. The aim is to socialise the student teacher into the profession and the profession's values. Teaching is located within a set of beliefs, values and traditions that are shared and understood by those already in the profession, but which are seldom articulated. You bring with you a unique personality and a set of attitudes, skills and preferences. Unquestionably, teachers already in post will influence the development of your professional and personal identities as student teachers.

The requirements of the Education Reform Act of 1988 place a duty on all teachers to promote the 'spiritual, moral, social' education of their pupils and yet the teacher training Standards in England make only passing reference to these areas. The determination of the government to uphold certain values, often expressed in platitudes has led to confusion about the expectations that are now being placed upon teachers. Sir Ron Dearing's revision of the National Curriculum 'successfully' excised practically all references to the values content of subjects;

this has resulted in reinforcing the assumption that what teachers need is more expertise in their subject specialisation. From this perspective, the values dimension of teachers' knowledge is either ignored or trivialised because it assumes that caring for pupils is an activity for which no special skill is required.

The characteristics that define teaching do not necessarily imply the criteria for good, successful or even effective teaching. Successful teaching is simply teaching which brings about the desired learning in narrow subject terms. Effective teaching is determined objectively by the nature of the subject itself and how best to teach it. Good teaching is harder to discern and is, therefore, open to wider interpretation. It has long been accepted that the definition of good teaching is much wider than merely the successful transmission of knowledge. The idea of the 'good teacher' takes on a richer hue if he or she is viewed as someone who is capable of expressing care and respect; who takes the pupils seriously and finds what is good in them. Teachers are often the victims of circumstance. External constraints often distort what teachers 'ought' to be doing. In a culture of Standards and technique teachers confuse authority with power – the two are not the same. When teachers depend on the coercive power of a set of techniques they have lost their authority. Teachers need to reclaim the authority of the teacher from the inside.

There has been a continuing fear among teacher educators that the Standards-based arrangements for initial teacher training (ITT) in the context of England and Wales simply continue to weaken the link between theory and practice. In the 1980s and early part of the 1990s the Council for the Accreditation of Teacher Education (CATE) was commissioned by the Department of Education and Science (DES) to improve teaching quality and it was given responsibility for advice about, and the specification and implementation of, the criteria which Initial Teacher Education (ITE) courses awarding QTS should meet. CATE concentrated its attention on three areas of teacher competence: (a) academic knowledge; (b) professional skills; and (c) personal qualities. Whilst (a) and (b) received detailed attention, (c) was presented in the form of some basic guidance on the requirements expected of candidates at interview. Her Majesty's Inspectorate (HMI) did comment on the qualities of good teachers by observing that reliability, punctuality, co-operation and a willingness to take on essential tasks were important. No attempt was made to define what was meant by personal qualities. Circular 24/89 specified five limited criteria for the personal qualities of potential candidates for teacher training: a sense of responsibility, a robust but balanced outlook, sensitivity, enthusiasm and a facility in communication. Circular 9/92, which established the competence-based system of teacher training, was widely seen by commentators as inadequately defining the complexities of professional values and expertise in two major areas: reflection, and moral and ethical judgements (see Arthur *et al.*, 1997). At the very end of the circular's list of competences, under the heading of Further Professional Development, it merely notes that student teachers should have a 'readiness to promote the moral and spiritual well being of pupils'. In 1997 the TTA issued new Standards (as opposed to competences for teaching) and for the first time there was a brief reference to the fact that teachers should 'set a good example to the pupils they teach, through their presentation and their personal and professional conduct' (Circular 4/98).

These developments tended to increase the scope of the debate about professional values and purposes in education but there still remained an overemphasis on the behavioural aspects in the competences/Standards. Pring (1992: 17) commenting on the older competences said that

> These conditions make little mention of theory. They require no
> philosophical insights. They demand no understanding of how children
> are motivated; they attach little importance to the social context in
> which the school functions – unless it be that of local business and
> the world of work; they attach no significance to historical insight into
> the present; they have no place for the ethical formulation of those who
> are to embark on this, the most important of all moral undertakings.

Pring is making the point that the ethical intuition of good teachers is frequently as important as their subject-area knowledge and teaching skill. Carr (1993a) has also noted that:

> The crude and artificial separation of competences from attitudes
> reinforces the false impression that what we are solely concerned
> with in the professional preparation of teachers is a kind of *training*
> in repertoires of uncontroversial skills and dispositions when what
> such preparation should be truly concerned with is the *education* of
> professional capacities to address rationally issues which, on any
> correct view of the logic of educational discourse, are deeply
> controversial and problematic.

Questions about a school's educational purposes are often neglected, as the focus is on cost effectiveness. There is a corresponding increase in the technical element of teachers' work and a reduction in the professional aspects, as schools and teacher education are increasingly regulated by external agencies.

The ethical dimensions of teaching

Teachers are still a major influence on pupils and the values they form. These values are reflected in what teachers choose to permit or encourage in the classroom – the way a teacher insists on accuracy in the work of pupils, or responds to their interests, conveys values which are clearly being introduced to those pupils. We know that research (Halstead and Taylor, 2000) strongly indicates that warm, positive and secure relationships between teachers and pupils aid learning. Teachers represent the school's philosophy to the pupil and the larger public. A teacher cannot be entirely *neutral*, for pupils need the example of those who are not indifferent. They need teachers who are full of enthusiasms and commitments in their teaching. All the time teachers are teaching they are under examination by their pupils. Their characters are analysed, their fairness is examined and their inconsistencies are probed. Teaching is clearly a test of character for a student teacher. The teacher is a model of what it is to be a human being for pupils and no amount of competence in the class will compensate if the teacher is not an appropriate model.

Teaching is a moral science, for as Elliott (1989: 9) proposes:

> When teachers are viewed as practitioners of an ethic then they may be described appropriately as members of a *profession*. But when their activity is viewed as a kind of technology then their status may simply be reduced to that of the technician.

In addition, Tom (1980) has concluded that:

> Teaching is moral in at least two senses. On the one hand, the act of teaching is moral because it presupposes that something of value is to be taught (Peters, 1965). On the other hand, the teacher–student relationship is inherently moral because of its inequality. This relationship, notes Hawkins (1973), entails 'an offer of control by one individual over the functioning of another, who in accepting this offer, is tacitly assured that control will not be exploitative but will be used to enhance the competence and extend the independence of the one controlled...'. Those who adhere to the applied science metaphor are insensitive to the moral dimension of teaching because their primary focus is on increasing the efficiency and effectiveness of teaching.

Teaching by this view is a moral craft. The adoption of a moral perspective on teaching does not, however, mean that one can abandon learning outcomes.

Much has been written in the area of values in teaching, not least by White (1990), who describes early education as the 'formation of dispositions'. Wilson (1993: 113) also speaks of moral dispositions when he says:

> Moral qualities are directly relevant to any kind of classroom practice: care for the pupil, enthusiasm for the subject, conscientiousness, determination, willingness to co-operate with colleagues and a host of

others. Nobody, at least on reflection, really believes that effective
teaching – let alone effective education – can be reduced to a set of
skills; it requires certain dispositions of character. The attempt to
avoid the question of what these dispositions are by emphasising
pseudo-practical terms like 'competences' or 'professional' must fail.

The argument here is that teachers must provide support for classroom learning which goes beyond the mere mechanics of teaching. Elsewhere, Eraut
(1994) argues that teachers have a moral commitment to serve the interests of
their pupils by reflecting on their well-being and their progress and deciding
how best these can be fostered. By doing this they contribute to the moral shaping
of their pupils. As Sockett (1993: 14) observes: 'many teachers have a moral vision,
a moral sense, and a moral motive however mixed up they may be in any
individual'. How much of this is recognised in teacher training? Elbaz (1992)
believes that we do not pay enough attention to this aspect of teacher education
and training as a result of our 'technocratic mind set'. Goodlad (1990) go further,
commenting that we need to address a fundamental void in the preparation
of teachers:

> Teaching is fundamentally a moral enterprise in which adults ask
> and require children to change in directions chosen by the adults.
> Understanding teaching in this light confronts a teacher with potentially
> unsettling questions: By what authority do I push for change in the lives
> of these children? At what costs to their freedom and autonomy? Where
> does my responsibility for these young lives begin and end? How should
> I deal with true moral dilemmas in which it is simply not possible to
> realise two goals or avoid two evils? How much pain and discomfort
> am I willing to endure on behalf of my student teachers? How are my
> own character flaws affecting the lives of others?

There is a need to consider how well students are currently prepared to meet
these questions.

There are many who believe that the present arrangements for teacher education
undermine the teaching profession and that it is time to reassert the professionalism
of teachers. Downie (1990), for example, believes that the teaching profession
should be seen as service through relationships and that teachers have a duty to
speak out on matters of social justice and social utility. He also believes that
teachers should be educated rather than trained, on the basis that educated
persons remain interested in their subject and think it worthwhile to pursue it,
the mechanics of teaching being no substitute for their knowledge. Hoyle and John
(1995) have said much about the responsibility of teachers which goes beyond
accountability or simply meeting the requirements of a set of procedures. With

regard to the qualities of a teacher, they list a number, professing that teachers should be: tolerant, patient, gentle, sympathetic, socially conscious and responsible. A danger, however, is the development of an 'omnicompetent model' of teaching in which the expectations of the teacher's role are extremely extensive.

Clearly, any view of ethics for teaching should have broad public and professional support. Nevertheless, teachers need to possess a set of virtues as the teacher's moral practice in teaching is something to be emulated. As Strike (1995) says, the way the teacher talks and behaves is taken by pupils as a basis for how they should behave. Carr (1993b) criticises teacher training competences for presenting teaching as a relatively value-free technological enterprise, concerned solely with the delivery of a prescribed curriculum. He believes that teachers should be viewed as 'better' people and have certain virtues. The difficulty here is that the virtues are often vague and may be almost meaningless within an educational context. A problem here may be the personal life of teachers, and whether this can conflict with their duties as teachers. He concludes that most problems in the professional sphere call for a 'moral rather than a technical response' and that practice needs to be characterised in 'terms of virtues rather than skills'. Clearly, this view places a considerable moral burden on teachers, of which student teachers will need to be aware.

What are the practices that will facilitate ethical Standards among teachers? The ethical dimension of teaching cannot be located in any particular element or at any specific moment of educational activity; rather, it should affect the whole person. It would be difficult for any one person to compile a list of practices that would be accepted by the teaching profession. Neville (1993) has compiled a Shared Values Charter for comprehensive schools in which each member of the school community is encouraged to respect, and use opportunities to serve, others. The Charter emphasises the equal value of all persons, openness, participation, co-operation, development of the whole person and empowerment. The Charter is rather broad and would need to be tailored to the circumstances of each particular school. However, professional values in teaching can be demonstrated through the teacher's respect for pupils as individuals. In the area of relationships with pupils for example, a whole series of ethical/value competences can be described. Teachers, including student teachers, will wish to inculcate honesty in pupils and will encourage them to tell the truth. Above all, teachers will always ensure that pupils come first; they will care for them and always try to find what is good in them; they will treat them seriously and consider their interests; they will help them gain self-respect and will understand in their teaching that pupils are often frightened by the level of difficulty of their work, and especially by the consequences of their inability to learn. Teachers will help pupils to make a real effort by consciously ensuring that they experience a sense of achievement. Teachers will listen to pupils, they will praise them, they will be available for them and will focus on their success. Teachers will be models of interpersonal relations.

Other value areas, which could be subdivided to create statements indicating what teachers should be expected to do, include: positive relationships with other teachers and parents; regard for equal opportunities and consideration for others; involvement with ethical issues and helping to resolve the value conflicts of pupils; commitment to professional development and developing a sense of professional judgement; a sense of responsibility for personal and collective actions and maintaining confidentiality – there are no doubt other areas which have not been outlined above. There is a case for student teachers explicitly illustrating at least a selection of these values during their school experience.

Chappell and Hager (1994) make the case that teacher competences which ignore values, including ethical and personal qualities, are worthless. They adopt an integrated approach to producing descriptions of practices which can capture the ethical and value positions of a profession. Values are posed as informal learning practices which characterise the initiation of new teachers into the teaching profession. Some of these are immeasurable but Chappell and Hager make a strong case for the assessment of values. They state that the idea of empathy for pupils in the abstract is difficult to describe and assess, but that in a classroom situation one could make a judgement. They propose that 'by describing attributes and activities in an integrated and contextualised way, long standing difficulties associated with arbitrary and idiosyncratic "hidden assessments" of individuals, which often have characterised values assessment in the workplace, can be avoided'. Further, they suggest that teachers should themselves compile lists of Professional Value Practices for the classroom and school.

A much more complex area involves the values dimensions of particular subject areas. Some subject areas have a more direct relationship to the question of values than do others, but none is exempt. Every subject teacher needs to be aware of the requirement to promote the betterment of their pupils and this can be achieved through curricular areas. In mathematics, for example, teachers might ask student teachers to consider: How are the examples they use constructed? What values are implicit in the contexts? Is there any bias in the example? Such 'values questions' encourage reflection on the moral aspects of teaching. In the same way the science teacher may ask student teachers whether they encourage pupils to consider the impact on society of scientific advancement.

The same might be applied to particular teaching methods. If subject teachers accept that there is a moral dimension to the teacher's role, then they may be able to suggest the nature of the values dimension in their subject area. For example, what may be effective teaching for some, say, teaching science at the learning pace of the most able, may at the same time be morally questionable for those who cannot keep up. It is these types of issues that student teachers need to consider and link to professional values. Another area for discussion might concern whether someone having a sound knowledge of their subject but no respect for what they are teaching is acceptable in the teaching profession. Do student teachers need to display a love of their subject?

Experienced teachers should be aware also that student teachers bring their own sets of values, attitudes and emotions to the school and to their teaching. Student teachers often show fear, and experience both failure and success in their teaching and staff relationships. In their contacts with pupils, student teachers can experience stress and show their anxiety. Teachers have a responsibility to support student teachers, especially in the early stages of their school experience. Experienced teachers, however, recognise that student teachers will need emotional maturity, which is linked inextricably to the acquisition of, and use of, classroom competences. They will ask: Are they adequate role models for the pupils? Are they patient with pupils? Are they selfish or generous with their time? How do they behave with other teachers? Student teachers' main example in attempting to answer these questions is often the subject teachers themselves. Again, the role of teaching places emphasis on the professional value commitments of subject teachers. This is why it is important that subject teachers, should not take their valuably acquired experience for granted. It is this openness which will encourage a professional relationship through which the student teacher will learn.

Reflective practice

In general, there have been two approaches to competence, described by Whitty and Willmott (1991). The first is that competence is seen as an ability to perform a defined task satisfactorily. Second, competence is seen as wider than the first formulation, encompassing attitudinal dimensions and professional values. In this second view neither the competence nor the criteria of achievement are so readily susceptible to discrete identification. Chapter 8 contains a fuller discussion of the idea of reflective practice.

The terms 'reflection' and 'critical reflection' are increasingly appearing in the descriptions of approaches to teacher education. They are commonly found in the Whiting et al. (1996) survey of teacher education. Many argue that reflection is an essential professional attribute. It should enable teachers to respond quickly and appropriately to changing circumstances and maintain a critical perspective on their teaching. Reflection in practice could be defined as the conscientious and systematic review of the aims, plans, actions and evaluation of teaching in order to reinforce effectiveness. The question, however, is not whether student teachers should be encouraged to reflect; it is what they should be encouraged to be reflective about. Bridges and Kerry (1993) insist that the values dimension of teaching should be a focus for student teachers, and warn against any model of reflection which 'ignores the role of experience in the development of the situational knowledge and value base which inform intelligent professional judgement'. Avis

(1994) believes that since the idea of the 'reflective practitioner' works within the notion of good practice it can, paradoxically, be reduced to a 'technicist' model, as the word 'practitioner' emphasises 'competence'. However, a case might be made against such analysis as the term clearly has its roots in the language of 'action research' and 'reflective practice'. Perhaps a more useful way to describe a reflective teacher might be *reflective professional*, wherein the use of 'professional' gives increased weight to values which surround, inform and are informed by 'reflection'.

The research by Tickle (1996) would indicate that student teachers reflect mainly on the technicalities of teaching performance, which is focused on problem-solving and developing strategies which 'work' in the classroom. He found that aims and values underlying practice barely entered the realms of reflective consciousness, let alone becoming subject to any scrutiny and critique. He concludes:

> If the predominant assumptions in teacher education systems, as
> well as among individual teachers, are about the need to achieve
> efficient performance in observable, 'workable' technical and clinical
> skills, then it may be that Schön's (1983) notion of reflective practice
> will remain limited to thoughts about procedural matters and the
> means of effective teaching. Or it may be used simply, as an implicit
> tacit aim. The more fundamental and educationally necessary focus
> on the purposes and values of education, including those of teacher
> education, may continue to elude not just these teachers but the
> teaching community in general.

It has been argued (Calderhead, 1987) that reflection among student teachers is often not 'critical' and can easily focus on simple descriptive evaluations of technical skills or processes. Elsewhere it has been claimed that reflective practice has become a hook on which many teacher education courses hang their own philosophy. And yet for Carr (1993c) 'it is impossible truly to formulate any serious policies in education without some rational moral reflection upon the goals of human flourishing to which it is directed. Such reflection is also, of course, an occasion for the development of attitudes which should express themselves in a real moral commitment to these goals.' He concludes that the knowledge which should properly inform the professional consciousness of the competent teacher is 'rooted in rational reflection about educational policies and practices and what is ethically, as well as instrumentally, appropriate to achieve them'. It is this which is often lacking in teacher education courses, for the research evidence would indicate that student teachers do not, on the whole, reflect on the values dimension of teaching at much length. It is important, therefore, that subject teachers keep the issue of reflection always before the student teachers for whom they are responsible. How can the teachers assist student teachers in this area?

Socrates believed that the role of education is to make people both intelligent and good. The aim of teacher education today is to prepare skilled teachers, with the emphasis on competence. Teachers should also foster the good, for education is intrinsically a moral activity. McIntyre (1981) calls our attention to Aristotle's *Ethics* as an alternative source for a rationale for moral education. In *The Ethics* Aristotle's voice is more than his own as he constantly asks, 'What do we say?' not 'What do I say?' This collective voice is that of the shared norms and values of society and contrasts sharply with the individualistic voice typical of our present time. Our inability to say 'we' in making moral prescriptions reflects a lack of a genuine moral consensus and sense of moral community. As we have already said, at the heart of education is the relationship between teacher and pupil and at the heart of any school community is the ability to speak for the community's shared values and moral norms.

McIntyre (1985) takes a pessimistic view of teaching in that he says: 'Teachers are the forlorn hope of the culture of Western modernity . . . for the mission [with] which contemporary teachers are entrusted is both essential and impossible.' It is impossible, he claims, because we have no Standards of rational objectivity and we have no agreement even on what Standards are. This argument has some force to it, but it does not mean that we should abandon our search for the values and standards of a good teacher. It is important that teachers and lecturers recognise the 'problematic nature of knowledge, of values and thus of the practice of education itself' (Kelly, 1995: 136) by examining their own practice in terms of its goals as well as its methods. If student teachers are to be inducted into a profession whose value commitments are explicit, a professional ethical code for teaching will be required. It also means that teacher competences, viewed and operated as instrumental tools, cannot be an acceptable basis for training or educating future teachers.

CONCLUSION

Hoyle (1995: 60) has commented that one view is that 'To be "professional" is to have acquired a set of skills through competency-based training which enables one to deliver efficiently according to contract a customer-led service in compliance with accountability procedures collaboratively implemented and managerially assured.' He admits that this definition may exaggerate the views of those who perceive teachers fundamentally as technicians, but Bonnett (1996) says it is not sufficient for teachers simply to say that this competence-based training model is inappropriate because it does not accord with their underlying conception of education. He says that it is precisely their underlying conception of education that is being called into question by the political powers that be.

The instrumental values contained in the Standards are designed to bring about a complete reorientation with regard to the fundamental values in education. The significance of the substitution of the word 'training' for 'education' in regard to teacher preparation has not yet emerged. There is a mood of distrust among teachers about government intentions in teacher education, and much else besides. Teacher training has certainly become more like a school-based apprenticeship in which there are dangers that theory is excluded and even reflection is limited to improving technical competences.

Whilst you need to be careful about any *imposition* of values in schools, you cannot avoid *values in teaching*. That is why it is important that the values in the act of teaching are clearly described and understood. Ultimately, it is the family which is the main social agency for helping young people, but the goals of a school inevitably will refer to character development even if such references are limited explicitly to encouraging pupils to strive for personal success and to being of service to the community. The ethic of the professional teacher is different from that of the parent, but, ideally, it should be seen as one which complements it.

Student teachers certainly need to question themselves about their motives for becoming teachers and to reflect on what they perceive to be professional conduct. This is, for many reasons, not least the perceived lack of an agreed moral consensus within British society. More broadly the difficulty lies in the fact that government has systematically sought to impose a model of 'good teaching', which is defined almost entirely in instrumental terms as the achievement of a set of measurable outcomes. This model sits uneasily with any other which takes 'education' to be a process of eliciting the balanced and harmonious development of children, not least in terms of their social, moral and spiritual development. It is very easy to envisage situations where these two models clash, in particular where marginalised pupils are concerned. Situations will arise where a student teacher may have to engage in serious moral reflection on how far compliance with the 'official model' may be taken, where it is damaging to the interests of the pupils concerned. This necessarily involves a risk to the career of the student teacher if taken as a fundamental critique of the 'measurable outcomes' worldview, and one which needs to be carefully considered.

TASKS

Mapping the Professional Values (1)

Use the Standards for Professional Values to map out how they relate to a week in your school teaching. Create a teaching diary and record how you address or encounter each of these Standards in school. Which Standard features most in your diary? Which features least? Why is this? What support does your mentor provide to assist you in meeting these professional Standards?

Mapping the Professional Values (2)

Consider the Standards for Professional Values within your teaching subject area. Do the Standards influence the way you teach your subject? In what ways, if any, do the Professional Value Standards help you become a more effective subject teacher? Do the Standards have any relevance to your subject area?

2 The Professional Ethics of Teachers

> despite persistent attempts . . . to conceive education as a relatively
> value-free technological enterprise concerned with the effective
> delivery of knowledge and skills to pupils via a quasi-scientific
> technology of pedagogy, it is still almost certainly less misleading
> to regard it as essentially a *moral* undertaking.
>
> Carr (1993b: 194)

What are the ethical challenges that teachers will face in their future careers? How can the prospective teacher be ethical when he or she does not know with any certainty what it is to be ethical? These are questions that courses in teacher education need to address. Teachers find that ethical dilemmas, by their very nature are not clear-cut. They can present themselves in schools as shapeless and difficult-to-grasp conundrums in response to which the teacher's immediate reaction is to ask a practical question – what should I do? These questions invariably have an intrinsic moral dimension and the answer to them is often not entirely a free choice on the part of the new teacher. They need to consider and take note of the teaching Standards and other education documents such as the aims of the National Curriculum and the Statement of Values of the National Forum on Education and the Community. Student teachers need to understand that there is clearly a value framework against which ethical judgements are made in education. Teachers are not and neither should they be value neutral in their conduct. When a teacher tells a pupil to stop shouting they are showing that they value the right over the wrong, the good over the bad. Teaching the difference between right and wrong is what teachers do much of the time despite the fact that society often blames teachers for failing to do exactly this. It is expected that the teacher will be trustworthy in the sense that they will not misuse sensitive information provided to them about children and parents, that they will keep confidences and will respect all they have dealings with.

Teaching is an ethical profession, it presupposes that something of value is to be taught and it is concerned with improving people – in other words, personal formation.

This would appear to suggest that the teacher must require a 'good character' if they are to shape the character of the young. Indeed, on this view it is possible to argue that they should have better motives than ordinary people. Teachers share the moral obligations of any ordinary person, but ordinary people, however decent, do not have any specific moral obligations of public service. This obligation to educate the young is not only morally good, but also a morally better motive than simply teaching in order to earn a wage. However, this does not make a teacher a better person and a teacher may fail to live up to these professional obligations. It is of course possible that many teachers do not enter teaching primarily from a motive of service to others. Carr (1993b: 195) makes a very interesting point when he compares a doctor with a teacher. He suggests that a doctor may be dishonest and spiteful as a person, but that none of this may matter to a parent seeking his or her expertise to treat their child successfully. In contrast, a teacher who is competent and has the best teaching skills available in the subject they teach but is known to be privately a liar may well cause the parent to have grave reservations about placing their child in his or her care.

First, you need to understand something of what is meant by ethics and morality in the context of teaching. Morality is about rules, principles and ideals which have the potential to guide the choices of our actions and which provide a basis for justifying or evaluating what we do. Ethics refers to the moral standards which apply to teaching as a profession. The term 'ethics' therefore refers to the characteristic values of teachers. It attempts to describe the way in which their values are expressed through the practice of their role. In this sense the study and practice of professional ethics deals with practical questions about teaching and learning. The value of professional ethics is in the fact that teachers study the ethical principles and practices of the teaching profession in order to discover how belonging to that profession entails discovering what is the proper way to act. The range of issues in teaching with ethical implications is immense. Ethics, for the teacher, involves both attitude and action. The former relates to the teacher's inner character or attitude as an ethical person: what one ought to become. Ethics for teachers will seek to motivate and guide them to become the best they can be as human beings. It should challenge teachers to be responsible and accountable for achieving certain attitudes and behaviours so as to achieve this ideal. The latter aspect of ethics for teachers is characterised by behaviour based on professional values and principles that enable teachers to evaluate and to amend their actions when they fall short of these values. How the teacher acts calls for choices to be made and this means being aware of the ethical dimensions of teaching and learning.

Friedman and Phillips (2003) define the model professional in three broad aspects: First, the model professional is also a model citizen as they obey the law and other generalised social norms for good citizenship. Second, the model professional is competent in his or her practice and third, the model professional is characterised by a set of behaviours which relate more to the manner in which they practise than the content of that practice. This third element appears to be based on the notion of the professional as possessing character. Traditionally, character was defined in terms of such attributes as honesty, chastity and virtue. These were seen as the chief guarantor of the integrity of professional conduct. At the end of the nineteenth century, current perceptions of the teaching profession emerged. Teachers were only selected for the role if they had appropriate characters, as it was considered that the example set by them was crucial. The teacher's role in schools was to inculcate specific social roles typified by a pattern of behaviour in children. The emphasis was on obedience and duty to all forms of authority in society and absolute conformity to predetermined social roles for the child. The teachers themselves were often not well educated and were selected for their ability to exhibit virtues in and outside of school. The overwhelming majority were women.

It is interesting to note that teaching is one of the last professional groups in England and Wales that has acquired a 'self-governing representative body' to regulate it. The legal, medical and nursing professions have all had long-established bodies which regulate entry, set minimum standards of professional knowledge and represent their members. Most importantly, each of them has the power to exclude a member from the profession not only on the basis of incompetence, but also for the violation of their code of professional ethics. Until very recently teachers in England have had no such professional body despite many calls for the establishment of one. In 1995 the Universities Committee for the Education of Teachers (UCET) conference set up a working party to formulate some Ethical Principles for Teaching. The working party outlined eleven principles that it claimed were fundamental to teaching and they are worth summarising here (Tomlinson and Little, 2000: 152–154):

ETHICAL PRINCIPLES

Teachers 'must':

1   have intellectual integrity;
2   have vocational integrity;
3   show moral courage;
4   exercise altruism;

5   exercise impartiality;

6   exercise human insight;

7   assume the responsibility of influence;

8   exercise humility;

9   exercise collegiality;

10   exercise partnership; and

11   exercise vigilance with regard to professional responsibilities and aspirations.

This list clearly demonstrates the ethical nature and obligations of teaching. Ethical issues are at the heart of teaching and are concerned with the way teaching is practised, organised, managed and planned. It is also inherently political because of the contested nature of teaching within the context of a State-sponsored education system. Another important point to stress is that a teacher loses some autonomy when he or she accepts membership of the teaching profession, for the teacher will need to demonstrate a commitment to the service of its general purposes.

The GTCE consulted the teaching profession about the Code and 77 per cent agreed that it represented the core beliefs, values and attitudes of the teaching profession. The introduction to the GTCE's new *Code of Professional Values and Practices* (2002) makes clear that the role of the teacher is 'vital, unique and far reaching'. It states that: 'This Code sets out the beliefs, values, and attitudes that make up teacher professionalism.' It is recognised that many who are attracted to the profession have a 'strong sense of vocation'. The introduction concludes by stating that the teaching profession works within the framework of the law and within the framework of equal opportunities for all 'respecting individuals regardless of gender, marital status, religion, colour, race, ethnicity, class, sexual orientation, disability and age'. Unlike the teaching Standards, the GTCE Code does not as yet have notes of guidance in the areas covered in the Code, but the GTCE are developing such notes and student teachers need to make themselves aware of them. The actual Code consists of six sections and describes the professional values that underpin the practice of teaching in English schools. The Code encourages productive partnerships with parents, governors, professionals and between teachers themselves. In relation to pupils the Code seeks high expectations on the part of teachers and expects them to demonstrate the characteristics they are trying to inspire in pupils, such as tolerance, honesty, fairness, patience and concern for others. The Code makes reference to helping to raise standards of achievement of pupils and in many respects is exactly like the Standards for teaching issued by the government.

The GTCE says they are produced as a source of encouragement for teachers and we have reprinted them below:

General Teaching Council for England Code of Professional Values and Practices

Young people as pupils

Teachers have insight into the learning needs of young people. They use professional judgement to meet those needs and to choose the best ways of motivating pupils to achieve success. They use assessment to inform and guide their work.

Teachers have high expectations for all pupils, helping them progress regardless of their personal circumstances and different needs and backgrounds. They work to make sure that pupils develop intellectually and personally, and to safeguard pupils' general health, safety and well-being. Teachers demonstrate the characteristics they are trying to inspire in pupils, including a spirit of intellectual enquiry, tolerance, honesty, fairness, patience, a genuine concern for other people and an appreciation of different backgrounds.

Teaching colleagues

Teachers support their colleagues in achieving the highest professional standards. They are fully committed to sharing their own expertise and insights in the interests of the people they teach and are always open to learning from the effective practice of their colleagues. Teachers respect the rights of other people to equal opportunities and to dignity at work. They respect confidentiality where appropriate.

Other professionals, governors and interested people

Teachers recognise that the well-being and development of pupils often depend on working in partnership with different professionals, the school governing body, support staff and other interested people within and beyond the school. They respect the skills, expertise and contributions of these colleagues and partners and are concerned to build productive working relationships with them in the interests of pupils.

Parents and carers

Teachers respond sensitively to the differences in pupils' home backgrounds and circumstances and recognise the importance of working in partnership with parents and carers to understand and support their children's learning. They endeavour to communicate effectively and promote co-operation between the home and the school for the benefit of young people.

The school in context

Teachers support the place of the school in the community and appreciate the importance of their own professional status in society. They recognise that professionalism involves using judgement over appropriate standards of personal behaviour.

Learning and development

Teachers entering the teaching profession in England have been trained to a professional standard that has prepared them for the rigours and realities of the classroom. They understand that maintaining and developing their skills, know-ledge and expertise is vital to achieving success. They take responsibility for their own continuing professional development, through the opportunities available to them, to make sure that pupils receive the best and most relevant education. Teachers continually reflect on their own practice, improve their skills and deepen their knowledge. They want to adapt their teaching appropriately to take account of new findings, ideas and technologies.

The Code is primarily a discussion document and the GTCE hope that it will have practical uses within schools. It is not a Code of Conduct and the GTCE make clear that 'This Code of Professional Values and Practice is therefore not a set of Standards against which teachers will be judged under the GTC's disciplinary powers nor is it appropriate for employers to use this Code in their own disciplinary procedures'. In order to analyse the Code it is useful to use the methodology of Friedman and Phillips (2003) since they developed five levels to reflect the degree of compulsion or coercion attached to a particular statement in a Code as follows:

> Level 1 signifies the highest degree of compulsion. It is the base level with an additional time perspective, e.g. Shall at all times, must always.
> Level 2 is the base level, e.g. shall, must, duty of care requires.
> Level 3 is a mid-point between Levels 2 and 4, or Level 4 with an additional time perspective e.g. should, ought, endeavour at all times.
> Level 4 is language that implies advice rather than compulsion and stresses the use of professional judgement as the advised action is clearly not applic-able to every circumstance, e.g. strive, it is preferable, shall endeavour.
> Level 5 applies to those statements that are presented as almost a statement of fact with minimal compulsion, e.g. asked, a member recognises.

By examining the GTCE's Code in terms of this structure it can be seen that it is written in language that requires the minimum of compulsion with the statements presented almost as fact: 'They are', 'Teachers recognise', 'They understand', 'Teachers support', 'Teachers demonstrate' and so on. There are no base level descriptions such as 'shall', 'must', or even 'should' or 'ought' in the Code. The Code has clearly been written as advice and encouragement to teachers, but how useful is it to student teachers and newly qualified teachers (NQTs) seeking concrete answers to what they should do? How can students put the Code into practice? The professional Standards use the same language as the Code and are very similar in content. The Code is not prioritised and is intended more as an aspirational document for teaching. As a result it is open to more than one interpretation. If the Code were written in a more exacting way then it would need to describe the context in which the words were used because of the complexity of the many situations in which teachers find themselves. The Code and the Standards do not provide the student teacher with guidance on how to discharge their day-to-day responsibilities in schools. The Code is not a set of rules – rather, it offers the teacher the opportunity to reflect on what it means to be ethical in teaching.

For example, school pupils are children who need to be regarded as persons in their own right with their own interests, abilities and personal characteristics. They are individuals capable of making choices and decisions. Teachers need to consider their feelings, their points of view and their differences when making judgements about them. Teacher judgements are integral to the work of teaching. Teachers will need to plan work for their pupils, will need to assess them and learn how to deal with them as people. Initially, the new teacher will be forced to make impressionistic judgements of their pupils. Such judgements, whilst made casually in the normal course of a day's teaching, can affect their motivation and self-image. And this in turn will impact on the pupil's performance in school. Teaching prospective teachers a set of skills that enable them to recognise the right course of action is only one answer. Another might be to enforce a Code of Professional Values and Practices that threatens poor teacher conduct with punishment. Professional ethics for teachers is not simply about Codes or Standards. It is necessary to derive the moral responsibilities of teachers from the nature of teachers as human beings and from the activity of teaching itself.

The Code does however speak about some obligations – the obligations that teachers owe to pupils, parents, the local community, to themselves, their colleagues and society. The Code indicates that teachers are expected to behave in a certain manner. The Code also attempts to display what the teaching profession wishes to project and a small list of virtues are provided. Nevertheless, the way in which the Code describes the norms and expectations of the profession is ambiguous and the strengths of the obligations owed to the stakeholders in educating the young are also unclear. The Code would not really assist the student teacher in prioritising these obligations. Most teacher education courses have long since abandoned offerings of moral education and ethics as a result of the pressures of time and limitations on the content of teacher education courses. Campbell

(2000: 219) commenting on teacher Codes in general remarks that: 'The real effect of a code in practice will likely be apparent in its interpretation, implementation, application, and, where necessary, enforcement rather than the code itself.'

The cultivation of virtues or dispositions does not normally form part of the discrete teacher education curriculum in higher education, rather it appears to form part of the hidden curriculum and relates to professional behaviour as sought by the Standards and the GTCE's Code of Practice. This Code seeks, in a general way, to help reinforce and inculcate the values and practices that are regarded as desirable for teachers. It is also the case that few lecturers in teacher education are trained in the teaching of professional ethics. It is rare for professional ethics to be taught separately but more often arises from within discussions in subject and professional education courses.

Yet generalised discussions about ethical matters leading to greater knowledge and understanding of ethical issues in teaching may not translate into ethical competence in schools. There is the question of the relationship between understanding and knowledge and their relevance to moral practice. We believe that a number of generalised objectives for learning and teaching across the teacher education curriculum can be outlined:

(a) An understanding of the GTCE's Code of Professional Values and Practices and how it is applied and the implications for defining professional conduct;

(b) An enhanced awareness of the ethical content of issues in teaching and learning;

(c) The ability to make ethical judgements and support them with reasoned argument;

(d) A desire to improve, enhance and refine one's professional behaviour; and

(e) How to evaluate the consequences of ethical guidelines with a view to their future modification.

You need to consider these ethical guidelines. You need to become critical professionals.

Some would say it is difficult to list the ethical principles that ought to inform teaching practice. McIntyre (1985) argues that a genuinely shared morality requires a justification in a shared conception of the purpose and meaning of human life. Without this, ethics are bound to lack universality and competing ethical theories will proliferate. McIntyre suggests we return to Aristotelian ethics of virtue as a solution. To this end Oakley and Cocking (2001) provide a promising approach to the ethics of professional roles by applying virtue ethics to professional practice. They argue that what counts as acting well in the context of the professional teaching role can be determined by how well that role functions in serving the goals of the profession – educating the young. Being a good teacher involves having appropriate dispositions, emotions and sensitivities in an educational context as well as performing appropriate actions. Which character traits count as virtues in teaching is determined by looking at what sort of dispositions help a teacher meet the goals of education. It was not so long ago that all new teachers would have been introduced to R.S. Peter's *Ethics and Education* and *Education and Responsibility* – each detailing the aims of education within an ethical context. The crowded teacher education curriculum today does not generally afford opportunities to study the philosophy of education. However, every new teacher should find time to at least read some pages of David Carr's *Making Sense of Education: An introduction to the philosophy and theory of education and teaching.*

Oakley and Cocking argue that good professional roles must be part of a good profession – one which has a commitment to a key human good. This good must play a crucial role in enabling us to live a flourishing human life. Teaching can be counted as such a profession as it is committed to promoting an important human good – education. Oakley and Cocking talk of the 'regulative ideal' meaning, in terms of teaching, that the teacher has internalised a certain conception of 'excellence' in such a way that he or she is able to adjust his or her motivations and conduct so that it conforms to that standard of 'excellence'. Here, we need to think of excellence in performing a function in terms of carrying out a role well. The regulative ideal of a good teacher must be determined by reference to some model of what teaching purports to be. This is of course informed by an account of the goals of education. As Oakley and Cocking (2001: 25) say: 'a regulative ideal is thus an internalised normative disposition to direct one's actions and alter one's motivations in certain ways'. They provide a very good example from Blum (1990: 176) who describes a secondary school teacher's (Herbert Kohl) experience of teaching reading to a fourteen-year-old boy:

> Kohl, then a secondary school teacher, was asked by some parents in a school in which he was teaching if he would give special tutoring to their son. The boy was 14 years old and did not know how to read. He was a large boy, angry and defiant; his teachers did not know how to handle him. Kohl agreed to work with the boy two days a week after class.
>
> Kohl worked with the boy for several months. Kohl found him extremely difficult and never grew to like him personally. But eventually he helped the boy to begin reading. Kohl describes how he came to take a personal interest in the boy's progress as a learner and to find satisfaction in what the boy was able to accomplish under his tutelage . . . [in deciding to help the boy] Kohl did not look at the situation in an impersonal way. He did not step back to adopt a standpoint reflecting a universal, impartial perspective, figuring out

what that standpoint urged on anyone situated similarly to himself...Rather, Kohl's motivation was of a more particularistic nature. He responded to, was moved by, the particular boy's plight, namely his being 14 years old and unable to read. Kohl experienced this as a terrible condition for the boy himself, and was aware of how damaged the boy would be if the schools system continued to be unable to teach him to read.

This story illustrates how a teacher guided by his concern *as a teacher* was motivated by the disadvantage of one of his pupils' inability to read. Kohl's conception of himself as a teacher clearly had an influence on how his decision to help the boy came about. For him the conception of the good teacher operated as a regulative ideal in his decision to take on the task of teaching the boy to read. He was not moved to help the boy as a friend – he did not like the boy – but rather *as a teacher* he sought to advance the boy's flourishing as a human being. He could not remain detached from the situation as his habits of acting as a professional teacher had become part of his character. The example shows that ethical thinking need not be consciously derived from ethical theories – and indeed that ethics should not be at the forefront of the teacher's mind, but rather part of their character. Kohl did not see his decision as arbitrary as this would have a paralysing effect on the pursuit of his professional commitment to the boy.

Blum's example is a good way of teaching ethics for it presents a case method approach. A real-life vignette is selected, depicting a situation in which ethical dilemmas arise. This can be used in a seminar within teacher education courses. Prospective teachers can also raise these issues as part of their professional studies and include them within their portfolios of teaching experience. The following are examples of the kinds of discussions or seminar-led topics that prospective teachers might consider worth pursuing.

TASKS

Ethical scenarios

In each of the following scenarios identify and comment on the ethical issues involved and consider your own response:

1   If you found that a colleague was showing considerable favouritism to a particular pupil;
2   You discover that a colleague is negligent or incompetent in a part of his/her role;
3   A colleague is seen stealing from a school fund;

4   You find that you have a conflict of interest in the school;
5   You believe a teacher is far too strict and uses excessive sanctions against his pupils; and
6   You are asked to follow a school policy that names pupils who have failed their exams in front of the rest of their class.

Teacher obligations

What are the obligations that a teacher owes to:

> Pupils?
> Parents?
> Headteacher?
> Profession?
> Local community?
> Themselves?
> Colleagues?

Teachers and virtues

Virtues are really taught by example and can be understood as an acquired disposition to do what is good – and in this sense the good is not something to reflect on, but is something to be done. The virtues are values that we embody, live and enact. Consider the following list of virtues or behavioural norms that are, in various educational contexts, expected of teachers:

Dignity	Integrity	Diligence	Loyalty	Honour	Truth
Courtesy	Love	Fairness	Moderation	Caring	Humility
Compassion	Sensitivity	Justice	Tolerance	Kindness	Responsibility
Respect	Enthusiasm	Flexibility	Reliability	Tact	Confidentiality

Now answer the following questions in relation to each separate virtue listed above.

> What does the virtue mean for you?
> Why should you practise it in teaching?
> How would you practise it in classrooms and schools?
> What would it look like in the context of teaching if you observed it?

Values and teaching

It is often argued that the promotion of moral values is the concern of all teachers qua educators. Consider the following quotation from the National Curriculum Council's document *Spiritual and Moral Development* published in April 1993:

> Values are inherent in teaching. Teachers are by the nature of their profession 'moral agents' who imply values by the way they address pupils and each other, the way they dress, the language they use and the efforts they put into their work.
>
> Does this extract provide you with any practical advice?
> Do you agree that teachers should be expected to exercise some positive influence over the quality of a pupil's attitudes and conduct?
> Do you think a teacher is a 'moral agent'? If so, in what way?

CONCLUSION

The General Teaching Council's Code is a welcome development and it is interesting that the Code as well as the TTA Standards are almost identical to the list produced by Campbell (2000: 214–215). It is vital that teachers do not think that because a professional Code has been agreed, there is no longer the duty to think about the ethical issues. The Code itself is not a set of operating rules and procedures – it requires teachers to make choices and decisions after reflecting on the principles as set out. Courses in teacher education need to encourage enhanced sensitivity of teachers not just to emphasise behavioural and technical skills. Teachers have special moral responsibilities because they are teachers. Good education is a basic precondition of the flourishing of each and every human being.

3   Values in the Classroom

The third of the QTS Professional Values and Practice Standards requires teachers both to *demonstrate* and to *promote* the 'positive values, attitudes and behaviour that they expect from their pupils'.

The word 'promote' is particularly important. Possessing certain professional values and attitudes is one thing; making them part of the 'fabric' of classroom practice, which is what promoting them involves, is quite another. However thoroughly teachers can claim to hold any proposed values at a purely personal level, what counts most in their professional practice is the extent to which they can successfully *apply* them in their work so that positive attitudes and dispositions inform and influence the ways that pupils work and learn. This means creating classrooms in which pupils themselves assimilate the desired values, and exhibit them in their own behaviour and approaches to their learning. It is through the course of a teacher's interactions with pupils, mainly in classroom teaching and learning (though also, of course, in interactions with them outside formal lessons), that a teacher both shows that he or she *demonstrates* these characteristics, and *promotes* them among pupils.

The *Handbook of Guidance* (TTA, 2003) sheds light on the kind of values 'which can be expected'. They include:

- respect for other people;
- positive attitude towards learning;
- respect for cultural diversity;
- care for the environment;
- social responsibility;
- positive relationships with pupils, particularly through positive communication;
- communication of attitudes, values and behaviour both explicitly and by personal example;
- lessons which motivate pupils and encourage them to engage in learning;
- establishing high expectations for pupil behaviour;
- resolving conflicts between pupils appropriately;

- encouraging a 'can do' approach;
- engaging with a school's values and respect for its ethos;
- implementing the school's policies on discipline, bullying or harassment; and
- demonstrating professional behaviour in areas such as time management and reliability.

This offers some useful starting points, but we will be noting other perspectives which extend and widen these suggestions. We will be concentrating in this chapter on what is involved for teachers in promoting positive values in the classroom, and in 'A Lesson Observed' one sample lesson will be analysed in some detail to see how this was achieved. We begin, though, by looking at values-based learning in schools and classrooms more generally. We look later at research perspectives which illuminate, respectively: the professional characteristics of effective teachers; dimensions of classroom 'climate'; the characteristics of effective learners; and, briefly, enabling young people to be active participants in their own development as learners.

At the end of the chapter there are tasks and investigations which will help you to take further some of the ideas and principles explored in it.

HEALTHY LEARNING ENVIRONMENTS AND VALUES-BASED LEARNING IN CLASSROOMS

A thread connecting all the bullet points above is the inescapable contribution made by everything a teacher is and does to establishing a classroom culture in which pupils respect and care for others, feel encouraged and motivated, and positively engage in learning. It is about the creation of a positive climate for learning in the classroom. There is no doubt that a key factor in establishing healthy learning environments in individual classrooms is the overall ethos and culture of the *whole school*, and that where a school has a powerfully driven and promoted system of core values it is easier for each individual teacher to 'feed' off this in creating their own positive classrooms. This is very clearly demonstrated in schools which have espoused a vigorously implemented values-centred approach. The whole organisational culture can certainly ease things for the individual teacher, and, of course, it can do exactly the opposite where the culture of a school is ill-defined or lacking positive direction. It would be wrong, though, to take the view that everything depends on the pre-existence of that whole school culture. Teachers can draw strength from the wider ethos of the school as a whole organisation, but it is ultimately individual teachers working in their own teaching spaces and with each group of pupils with whom they interact who turn the aspirations of a school policy into actual practice. Every teacher bears individual responsibility for making their classrooms ones in which positive values are *explicitly* promoted.

That word 'explicitly' is critical. For rather too long we have perhaps been a little complacent about addressing these matters head-on and deliberately. A theme which runs through all the work on effective learning is the central importance of involving pupils directly and openly in appreciating and understanding the values, concepts and principles we are considering here. Evidence is growing that the more explicit teachers are about naming, defining and sharing with pupils the values they want to promote *as a normal and routine part of lessons*, making this a central and overt concern in all teaching and learning (and ever-present in all aspects of school life), then the more those values take root and influence classroom climate and hence the overall culture of the school. The formulations of Curriculum 2000 and National Strategy initiatives have helped to place attention on 'Key Skills' and generic features of effective learning, including values. This has been complemented by new emphasis on preparing the ground for 'lifelong learning' in which the values and attitudes that learners attach to the act of learning are central.

There are now many examples of classrooms in which pupils are being formally and explicitly guided and trained in how to think, talk and write about their own learning as a normal part of each lesson. They are classrooms in which key principles such as honesty, respect, trust, justice and love of learning are openly nurtured. Teachers have found ways of successfully accommodating these vital elements of truly educative practice within the formal regulatory requirements in which schools work. The subject of learning itself or 'learning to learn' is increasingly being recognised as a necessary focus of explicit attention, as part of the overt rather than the 'hidden' curriculum. Powerful and productive work is being done in many schools, even with children in the earliest stages of formal education. They are being helped towards self-awareness of themselves as learners, and being encouraged to acquire and use the language of values just as they acquire the specialised vocabularies of traditional curriculum disciplines and subjects. In a Year 5 class in a primary school which is part of a values development pilot project supported by the Local Education Authority (LEA) and a local university, pupils have generated their own list of core values which underpin their lives and work – both in school and at home. A section of the wall display is devoted to it, and among more than thirty on the list are:

happiness
kindness
helpfulness
friendship
freedom
importance of family
personal expression
thinking
thoughtfulness

creativity
relationships
respect
hope
applying knowledge
justice
celebrating talents
trust
peace
belief
truth
pride
sharing
strength
comfort.

The display is not just symbolic. Observing the pupils at work (which includes lessons devoted quite specifically to values), you can see and hear them making reference to and acting on these principles. While this school is going further than some in putting values education into the mainstream curriculum, there are countless examples of schools in which the classroom walls display guiding principles agreed at institutional or class level.

BRINGING COGNITIVE AND AFFECTIVE INTERESTS TOGETHER

It is important to recognise that making values the centre of classroom life involves quite radical re-thinking about the relationship between what we know as the *cognitive* and *affective domains* of education since Bloom's and others' definitions of them (Bloom, 1956; Krathwohl *et al.*, 1964). 'Cognitive' refers to objectives predominantly involving 'knowing', while 'affective' refers to those 'which emphasise a feeling line, an emotion, or a degree of acceptance or rejection' (Bloom *et al.*, 1971). For rather too long the two domains have been held apart, and it could well be said that the cognitive domain has had priority. That tendency is still present in the emphasis on raising standards of achievement which almost exclusively reflect cognitive objectives. Significantly, as the rate of improvement in these standards has levelled off and achieving higher targets has proved increasingly elusive, more and more attention is being devoted to why this should be so. Some of the answers are being sought in factors which lie much more in the affective domain such as pupils' attitudes to schooling, feelings about being learners, the extent to which (in Bloom's words) they feel 'accepted' or 'rejected' in lessons, and their general motivation. There are other reasons why values and attitudes have entered the school curriculum with new energy, of course, which have more to do with wider social, political and economic concerns. We will be returning briefly to this later.

The impact that learners' attitudes and dispositions towards learning have on educational achievement is fundamental. There is increasing recognition that values, attitudes and dispositions on the one hand, and knowledge, skills and understanding on the other, interrelate with and interpenetrate each other, and that the two domains must be developed in parallel. Bart McGettrick (in an as yet unpublished conference paper) provides a usefully visual conceptualisation of this interconnection in borrowing James Watson's and Francis Crick's seminal 1953 'double helix' model of DNA, in which the two domains intertwine:

Source: McGettrick, 2002

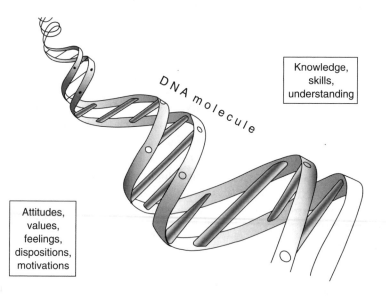

Just as the model unlocked the secrets of DNA, we suggest that it has equivalent power in assisting teachers to see the need to merge attention to both cognitive and affective domains. Conceptualising the interrelationships between the two strands is one thing. Planning lessons which succeed in putting a synthesis between them into action is the next step. Actually managing lessons which achieve the synthesis is another challenge altogether.

A LESSON OBSERVED: VALUES IN PRACTICE

It is relatively easy to identify the values we want to promote in classrooms, as the guidance supporting QTS Standard 1.3 does. The real trick is to make them an integral part of classroom practice. What does a lesson that achieves this look like? What techniques, strategies and teaching and learning events characterise a classroom in which a strong focus on knowledge, skills and understanding is matched by an equally strong focus on positive values, attitudes and behaviour among pupils? How do teachers put values-based teaching and learning into practice? Observing expert classroom practitioners at work goes a long way towards helping us – at whatever stage we are in our own professional development – to see more clearly the possibilities and opportunities. What follows is a pen-portrait of an actual lesson which very largely achieved the synthesis we are talking about, where attention to the subject matter in the scheme of work was matched by parallel attention to structures and processes, and 'frameworks for learning' supporting the development of positive attitudes and dispositions to learning. At the end of the lesson, the abiding impression was that pupils had learned as much about *how* to work and learn effectively as they had about the topic itself. Telling the story of a lesson is no substitute for being present and observing first-hand, but this portrait of a lesson illuminates clearly what is really meant by such things as 'social responsibility', 'communication of attitudes, values and behaviour both explicitly and by personal example' and 'encouraging a 'can do' approach'.

The class was a Year 8 mixed-ability class in a school in a small town with a rising population whose intake comprised children from both urban and rural areas. The class included pupils with special educational needs who receive extra support of various kinds. The story of the lesson is divided into eight phases for analytical purposes, with some key points highlighted as bullet points. Many of these points connect directly with the list of values with which we started. We suggest that these are the kinds of features which you might be looking out for, both in your own lesson observations of other teachers, and in managing your own classrooms.

A LESSON OBSERVED

Phase 1: Meeting and greeting

It was the lesson after morning break, and the teacher was able to reach the classroom before the children arrived. She stood by the door as they entered, greeting individual pupils as they came in. She settled them into their places, occasionally directing a pupil to a particular place, making sure that each pupil was preparing for the lesson, which included taking coats off and putting bags on the floor. She greeted them again, formally addressing the class as a whole.

- establishing (or re-establishing) personal rapport;
- occupying the 'territory' of learning as its controller;

- setting the physical conditions for learning; and
- moving quickly from a fairly informal 'greeting' role to a formal 'teaching' and leadership role in the opening interaction.

Phase 2: Establishing routines

She called for complete silence for the register. She will know from this, with certainty, which pupils were absent from that lesson, circumventing any nonsense from any who claim later that they cannot do something because they were not present, and providing information about those who might need special help because they really were absent. Once or twice some pupils started chatting during the register. She stopped immediately and quietly repeated her insistence on silence, speaking decisively but not loudly. Her tone and body language communicated authority, and she received respect from the talking children.

- organisational routine, well understood by all;
- authority and presence achieved without histrionics;
- sanctity of protocols; and
- patience and non-escalation.

Phase 3: Mapping the lesson

After the register she presented an overview of the lesson, briefly describing the purposes and intentions of the work. She was sharing her aims and intentions with the pupils, and making her plan and her expectations completely explicit. It included reminding the class about work they had done in the previous lesson. She wrote on the blackboard a simple list of the four phases she had planned for the lesson. Pupils had a clear 'map' of what was ahead of them. This list stayed on the board. She ticked each one off as it was completed, drawing their attention to the next phase. Pupils could therefore keep track of where they were in the lesson, and had a strong sense of progress as each phase was ticked off. The lesson was a purposeful journey for the pupils: they could see the destination and the route, and they could 'place' their own progress in relation to its structure. They immediately became participants in the structure of the lesson and the map of the learning process – not just spectators at some ritual whose form they only vaguely, if at all, understood.

- publishing and sharing with pupils teaching and learning intentions;
- making aims and objectives explicit;
- setting expectations;

- providing an overview or preview;
- encouraging pupils to be informed participants in the lesson;
- signalling specific lesson components and progress through them; and
- giving pupils the means of understanding the structure, purposes and shape of the lesson.

Phase 4: Linking with previous learning

Next followed a short test which made connections with what they had done in the previous lesson. There were only eight questions, but each required a slightly different answering technique: recall of a key word; a short definition; a response needing a bit of imaginative, lateral thinking; one requiring an example of a technical nature, and so on. Some were easier than others, but they did not get progressively more difficult. There was no sense of some pupils having to 'give up' before the end because of increasing difficulty.

- continuity with and progression from prior learning;
- recall and reinforcement of prior learning;
- accountability for prior learning;
- clear and familiar task to maximise engagement right at the start of the lesson;
- making subject matter accessible to all pupils;
- differentiation for ability range;
- exercising different kinds of thinking and response; and
- challenge.

Phase 5: Encouraging responsibility for own learning

Pupils exchanged books and marked each other's answers, led by the teacher. Once or twice alternative answers were offered by pupils, and were approved or rejected by the teacher, encouraging individual initiative and offering some flexibility in terms of 'correctness', within limits. Scores were collected orally, and recorded in the mark book. They ranged from three to eight. The teacher made encouraging praising comments to three pupils when hearing their scores. What was noticeable was the total absence of any display of competitiveness. This was clearly a well-established routine, and there was simply no point in either cheating or making silly remarks about low (or high) scores.

- collaboration and co-operation;
- independence and trust;

- initiative and responsibility;
- immediate feedback on performance;
- selective encouragement through targeted praise; and
- positive reinforcement.

Phase 6: Building new learning

The test phase was ticked off on the blackboard agenda, and the lesson moved to the next phase. This involved revisiting material introduced in the previous lesson, but with a different purpose, and with the addition of new material for comparison. The strong feature of this was the way the teacher broadened and extended pupils' knowledge and understanding of the familiar material. It was the point in the lesson when they were really being made to think creatively. Some ideas were just beyond most of the pupils, but she supported their movement towards them by demonstrating and modelling ideas on the blackboard. She took ideas from the pupils themselves in careful questioning, and enlarged or refined them as she published them on the board. It was a classic example of working with learners in the 'zone of proximal development' (Vygotsky, 1978): that critical area for learning which each learner can reach – with the right kind of support. As Vygotsky says, 'The only "good learning" is that which is in advance of development.' There was a very strong sense of the class building something together, almost as a team, demonstrating a particular kind of 'social responsibility'. It was a kind of brainstorming session, but heavily structured and very tightly controlled. The teacher was training the class in a particular technique, by modelling and demonstrating the process with them, so that at a later stage pupils would be able to use the technique independently. In essence, it was a planning technique: a technique supporting higher-order levels of thinking. It was also a strategy helping pupils to conceptualise the learning activity ahead of them. By the end of this, the pupils were all in a position to start a period of private, independent work. The ideas had been gathered; there was a rich store of ideas to work with, and the learning tools to apply to them. They had been given a start and had a clear view of what was expected.

- building on and extending prior learning;
- working from the familiar to the unfamiliar;
- demonstrating and modelling a technique for learning;
- tutored collaborative rehearsal of a technique before 'going solo';
- moving from dependence on the teacher (and each other) to independence;
- training in how to learn;
- security and confidence in a specific learning process and activity; and
- practice in gathering and using ideas arising from co-operative effort.

Phase 7: Promoting independence, initiative and engagement in learning

At this point there was a phase of quiet private engagement on the task. The teacher moved around the class, monitoring levels of application discreetly and providing help to individuals. But her main role was very clear: she was ensuring that the right conditions for this kind of independent work were being maintained. Most of the time she was 'policing' the classroom 'at a distance', checking, listening, giving pupils the protection from each other that would help them to work at their best. This is vitally important, because we know only too well that many children do not have access to these conditions at home. It is very much every teacher's responsibility to 'train' children in working in a disciplined and applied way if positive attitudes towards learning are to grow. It may be the biggest service a teacher can give to a child. If the habits of responsible and disciplined work are developed under controlled conditions like this, there is a chance that each child will become an increasingly powerful learner. But the habits of 'learning to learn' have to be deliberately developed. They do not develop on their own.

- creating and maintaining conditions for effective engagement in learning;
- encouraging and supporting independence; and
- developing effective individual (and lifelong) habits of learning/working.

Phase 8: Reinforcing, reviewing and conceptualising learning

The pupils' independent work did not last long – just long enough to set a pattern for that kind of activity. They will return to build on the experience another time. They could also effectively continue in homework, given appropriate home conditions, since by now under the teacher's supervision there was clear understanding about not only *what* was to be done, but also *how* to do it. (How many homeworks are rendered near-pointless because pupils have very uncertain pictures of both aspects?) The teacher interrupted the task to move the lesson into its final phase devoted to feedback and review. The review gathered together the lesson's key points, concentrating on the whole picture rather than the details. This was true 'metacognition': developing conceptual understanding, knowing about knowing, getting the 'big picture', exercising higher-order skills, being challenged to see meaning and connections among parts in the whole. Finally, before an orderly dismissal which mirrored her meeting and greeting at the start, the teacher offered some general positive comments about the quality of the class's work in the lesson, especially in relation to the level of concentration they had maintained and the way pupils had involved themselves purposefully in the various parts of the lesson.

- reinforcement of learning;
- organising knowledge (about both 'substance' and 'techniques') for conceptualisation and recall;
- relating parts to the whole and 'mapping' understanding;
- qualitative appraisal of attitudes towards learning;
- valuing and celebrating positive working behaviour;
- enhancing motivation; and
- developing reflective learning.

One interesting aspect of this lesson was the almost total absence of any challenging misbehaviour by pupils. A class of perfect goody-goodies? No. There are two main reasons why the lesson was untroubled by misconduct. First, the teacher's personal organisation and planning for the lesson was extremely strong – and completely evident to the class. There were no weak spots in terms of structure or content which some pupils might have been tempted to exploit. Allied to this was the teacher's decisiveness – even assertiveness – in driving the lesson along with confidence, and with sufficient changes of activity to sustain pupils' interest, all fully prepared for and guided. A lot more could be said about the technical and professional skills which are the components of such teaching: command of verbal communication with children; mastery of material and an understanding of learning theory; a very clear sense of what 'being in charge' means; mental agility and energy, to indicate just a few. Second, what was very obvious was the quality of the rapport between the teacher and the class, in which there were high levels of mutual trust and respect which permitted pupils to feel confident themselves in working with her and with each other. It is certain that this is the product of consistent work over a period of time, through which certain patterns of behaviour and expectation have been carefully established, adjusted, developed and reinforced. That the pupils were fully prepared to go with this was, in great measure, due to their appreciation that this teacher was genuinely interested in them as individuals, enjoyed being with them and found ways of showing it, and, when appropriate, gave them controlled space and conditions in which to 'find' themselves as learners making positive progress.

If we go back to that list of values which the Year 5 class had on the wall, we can see many of them being reflected in this Year 8 class's work in the secondary school. The lesson clearly *demonstrated* and was *promoting* values and principles such as: helpfulness, personal expression, thinking, respect, applying knowledge, celebrating talents, trust, pride, sharing, comfort...and freedom. Freedom to work and learn; freedom from oppression by other pupils – or by the teacher.

RESEARCH PERSPECTIVE 1: PROFESSIONAL CHARACTERISTICS

This portrait of one lesson provides a picture of what demonstrating and promoting positive values actually looks like in practice. What further insight is there into factors which have been identified as contributing to healthy classroom climates, and to promoting positive attitudes towards learning? For this we need to turn attention to examples of research in order to get a broader picture of features which may not have been prominent in this single lesson. The Hay McBer study of teacher effectiveness is a useful starting point (Hay McBer, 2000). This study was commissioned by the then Department of Education and Employment 'to help take forward the proposals in the Green Paper *Teachers: meeting the challenge of change*' (DfEE, 1998). The research set out to 'create a vivid description of teacher effectiveness, based on evidence of what effective teachers do in practice at different stages in the profession'. The interest in 'different stages in the profession' was very much linked to the Green Paper's proposals, now in place, relating to 'modernising' the teaching profession, 'performance management' and the appraisal of teachers for progression beyond the main professional grade: 'Threshold' appraisal, and 'Advanced Skills Teachers'. This takes the Hay McBer study's remit well beyond the realm of initial teacher education, but the study provides, nevertheless, an important snapshot of contemporary thinking about some key features of effective teaching which are helpful to us here.

The Hay McBer study is concerned with elucidating three aspects of effective teaching: professional characteristics, teaching skills and classroom climate. We will look briefly at professional characteristics and classroom climate. The relevance of these to the issues explored in this chapter is clear from the study's opening remarks:

> The three factors are different in nature. Two of them – professional characteristics and teaching skills – are factors which relate to what a teacher brings to the job. The professional characteristics are the ongoing patterns of behaviour that combine to drive the things we typically do. Amongst those things are the "micro-behaviours" covered by teaching skills. Whilst teaching skills can be learned, sustaining these behaviours over the course of a career will depend on the deeper seated nature of professional characteristics. Classroom climate, on the other hand, is an output measure. It allows teachers to understand how the pupils in their class feel about nine dimensions of climate created by the teacher that influence their motivation to learn.
>
> (Hay McBer, 2000: 7)

We can align 'what a teacher brings to the job' – 'professional characteristics' – with QTS Standard 1.3's requirement for teachers to *demonstrate* certain characteristics; and we can align 'dimensions of climate created by the teacher' – 'classroom climate' – with the other key verb in the Standard: *promote*.

Hay McBer identifies 15 'professional characteristics' divided into five groups. The language is rather different from that used in *Qualifying to Teach* but, more importantly, the list offers a more systematic *conceptualisation* of a wider range of essential attributes, each of which carries with it certain assumptions about Professional Values and Practices. We should note that this categorisation of characteristics includes some (like 'Flexibility' and 'Teamworking') which are addressed or implied in various QTS Standards. Nevertheless, it is valuable to have this holistic perspective to complement the way the Standards deal separately with some of these issues.

Professional Characteristics (Hay McBer, 2000: 21–26)

Professionalism	Challenge and support	A commitment to do everything possible for each pupil and enable all pupils to be successful.
	Confidence	The belief in one's ability to be effective and to take on challenges.
	Creating trust	Being consistent and fair. Keeping one's word.
	Respect for others	The underlying belief that individuals matter and deserve respect.
Thinking	Analytical thinking	The ability to think logically, break things down, and recognise cause and effect.
	Conceptual thinking	The ability to see patterns and links, even when there is a lot of detail.
Planning and Setting Expectations	Drive for improvement	Relentless energy for setting and meeting challenging targets for pupils and the school.
	Information seeking	A drive to find out more and get to the heart of things; intellectual curiosity.
	Initiative	The drive to act now and pre-empt events.
Leading	Flexibility	The ability and willingness to adapt to the needs of a situation and change tactics.
	Holding people accountable	The drive and ability to set clear expectations and parameters and to hold others accountable for performance.
	Managing pupils	The drive and the ability to provide clear direction to pupils, and to enthuse and motivate them.
	Passion for learning	The drive and an ability to support pupils in their learning, and to help them become confident and independent learners.
Relating to Others	Impact and influence	The ability and the drive to produce positive outcomes by impressing and influencing others.

Teamworking	The ability to work with others to achieve shared goals.
Understanding others	The drive and ability to understand others, and why they behave as they do.

We suggest that this is a useful checklist when undertaking lesson observations. What examples of these characteristics can you see in observed lessons? What specific teaching and learning strategies and events provide *evidence* of them in operation? Look back at 'A Lesson Observed' and see whether you can match features which were described there to some of these more generically expressed characteristics.

Going a little further, consider for a moment the two aspects of 'Thinking' in the Hay McBer list: 'analytical' – breaking things down, and 'conceptual' – seeing patterns and links. Taking a particular topic which would form the substance of one lesson, how would you plan for both of these with, say, a Year 7 class?

One further practical exercise, this time relating to 'Flexibility'. Using an occasion from your own teaching experience when you were aware that you either *did* or *did not* 'adapt to the needs of a situation and change tactics', why did you decide the way you did, and what were the consequences? Would you, with hindsight, make a different decision now, in order to achieve a different outcome in terms of learners' engagement or achievement?

RESEARCH PERSPECTIVE 2: CLASSROOM CLIMATE

The Hay McBer study offers nine dimensions of Classroom Climate, defining it as:

> the collective perceptions by pupils of what it feels like to be a pupil in any particular teacher's classroom, where those perceptions influence every student's motivation to learn and perform to the best of his or her ability.

The dimensions are:

Classroom Climate (Hay McBer, 2000: 27–28)

Clarity	around the purpose of each lesson. How each lesson relates to the broader subject, as well as clarity regarding the aims and objectives of the school.
Order	within the classroom, where discipline, order and civilised behaviour are maintained.

A clear set of Standards	as to how pupils should behave and what each pupil should do and try to achieve, with a clear focus on higher rather than minimum standards.
Fairness	the degree to which there is an absence of favouritism, and a consistent link between rewards in the classroom and actual performance.
Participation	the opportunity for pupils to participate actively in the class by discussion, questioning, giving out materials and other similar activities.
Support	feeling emotionally supported in the classroom, so that pupils are willing to try new things and learn from mistakes.
Safety	the degree to which the classroom is a safe place, where pupils are not at risk from emotional or physical bullying, or other fear-arousing factors.
Interest	the feeling that the classroom is an interesting and exciting place to be, where pupils feel stimulated to learn.
Environment	the feeling that the classroom is a comfortable, well-organised, clean and attractive physical environment.

We might, perhaps, add one more dimension. It is certainly the case that if you ask children why some teachers make lessons interesting and motivating, time and time again they will put 'fun' at the top of the list. This is, however, a slightly risky concept, and it is easy to see why it has not found its way into a report like the Hay McBer study. We would propose, though, that the descriptor for 'Interest' should perhaps be: 'the feeling that the classroom is an interesting, exciting *and enjoyable* place to be...', and that somewhere in any list of professional characteristics should be included: 'a sense of humour'. The Year 5 primary class's wall display list of values included 'Ability to play' and 'Enjoyment'.

RESEARCH PERSPECTIVE 3: CHARACTERISTICS OF EFFECTIVE LEARNERS

Research and development work in schools at the University of Bristol in association with the Lifelong Learning Foundation is shedding fresh light on ways in which pupils see themselves as learners, and identifying the characteristics of effective learners. This moves us more explicitly towards the deliberate teaching of learning skills, but in the sense that QTS Standard 1.3 is very much about promoting motivation for learning it is appropriate to include insights from this work here. The Effective Lifelong Learning Inventory (ELLI) is a questionnaire for children 'about how we learn, about our feelings about learning and about the ways in which we can find out how to be better learners'. It comprises a series of statements which children rate on a continuum from 'Almost never true for me' to 'Nearly always true for me', from which a unique personal profile of 'learning power' (Claxton, 1999) can be derived. The profile represents graphically each learner's pattern of strengths and development areas in relation to seven dimensions of 'learning power':

Growth orientation;
Critical curiosity and energy;
Meaning making;
Creativity;
Resilience;
Positive learning relationships; and
Strategic awareness.

ELLI profiles are of individual pupils. This provides interesting information which can be used in diagnostic and formative ways in addressing their particular specific needs, but by analysing the profiles of a group or whole class it is also possible to 'map' the underlying characteristics of the group. In the words of the ELLI team:

> It may be that a group of learners turns out to be relatively low on strategic awareness, curiosity and making meaning. Then the teacher can use this information to facilitate learning opportunities that begin to develop more awareness, curiosity and higher order thinking.
>
> (ELLI, 2003)

The research is proving to be a very useful tool for teachers in identifying areas in which to direct attention, particularly in terms of developing positive attitudes and dispositions towards learning. As one teacher says:

> 'ELLI' has completely altered my feelings about teaching. I feel I can now teach learning skills quite explicitly, or at the very least expose pupils to situations where they can develop them. Before I felt that learning was more a set of skills which you either had or you didn't and that I could promote them simply by talking about the importance of listening, working together well, trying hard etc. I now feel I can support my pupils immeasurably more in taking responsibility not just for the work they do, but for how they do it. I feel I can get them to work at developing, for example, resilience, building up that skill from week to week. I feel that I am no longer a teacher just of English but a teacher of learning as well. This is incredibly positive. Throughout my teaching career I have told my classes that the whole point of education is to make them think for themselves and become better learners. I now have begun to understand how to teach them to do this, rather than just hope that it happens along the way.
>
> (ELLI, 2003)

The last sentence is highly relevant to the intentions behind QTS Standard 1.3. We began this chapter by noting that the Standard expects teachers both to demonstrate *and* to promote certain fundamental values, attitudes and behaviour. Here is clear evidence of one set of tools which is helping teachers to be purposeful and systematic about promoting positive attitudes to learning in their everyday work, and to translate what can otherwise be very generalised and abstract articles of professional faith into planned teaching and learning activities.

RESEARCH PERSPECTIVE 4: EMPOWERING LEARNERS

Much of this chapter has been about intepreting one specific QTS Standard as setting out requirements which look towards empowering learners. We mean by this a wide range of teaching strategies, beliefs about education, professional values and attitudes towards working with young people which have the common end of enabling them to be participants in their own development as learners, and to be knowledgeable about the processes they are engaged in as learners. Implicit in all these strategies, beliefs, values and attitudes is a host of specific professional skills: lesson planning, knowing the pupils, commanding appropriate registers of discourse with them, building positive relationships, knowing how to lead and assert authority in positive ways, and attending to fundamental aspects of pupils' development which go beyond the immediate concerns of the topic of the moment.

 None of this is easy, and none of it can be accomplished within the limits of a period of initial professional training. It is clear enough from the remarks of the experienced teacher about ELLI that it is a career-long journey. Teachers should not feel discouraged if achieving some of their ambitions relating to positive values-based education proves difficult. We have a long way to go before the educational system in which we work offers sufficient recognition of the importance of values over and against short-term outcomes and marginal improvements in attainment scores. Barbara McCombs, in the University of Denver Research Institute, draws attention to this in the course of her work on learner-centred teaching (McCombs, 2002: 3). She asks of the emphasis she sees around her on standards, assessment and accountability:

> is this the best focus? Many would argue not – particularly in light
> of crises that have surfaced in our nation's schools. These crises are
> outside the academic standards, achievement, and accountability arena,
> but they are clearly magnified as a result of the focus on this arena.
> They include youth violence in schools, suicide, depression,
> hopelessness, and alienation from learning – and the rising evidence
> of teacher stress, feelings of overwhelm and despair, and departure
> from the profession.

This is uncompromising language, but the symptoms are not confined to her nation's schools. We have to recognise that there is parallel alienation from learning amongst pupils in our own schools, and teacher stress and departure from the profession are major issues in our own educational system.

McCombs's (2002: 4) vision is for a re-alignment of thinking which balances learner needs with high standards of performance for all learners. Critical in this are 'educational models...that reconnect learners with others and with learning – person-centred models that also offer challenging learning experiences'. Real-life learning, she writes,

> is often playful, recursive and non-linear, engaging, self-directed, and meaningful from the learner's perspective. But why are the natural processes of motivation and learning seen in real life rarely seen in most school settings? Research shows that self-motivated learning is only possible in contexts that provide for choice and control. When students have choice and are allowed to control major aspects of their learning (such as what topics to pursue, how and when to study, and outcomes to achieve), they are more likely to achieve self-regulation of thinking and learning processes.

The elevation of student choice and control about what, how and when to study is probably not something we can fully support, except possibly as occasional luxuries, but the emphasis she places on more general aspects of self-regulation of thinking and learning processes lies at the heart of what we have been discussing. We would want to end by recommending, though, that this is *not* something that children can achieve without very deliberate *teaching*. What QTS Standard 1.3 is about is teachers creating the circumstances and conditions in which students can increasingly take responsibility for their own learning, *under skilled guidance*, through the gradual acquisition and assimilation of key values, attitudes and dispositions towards learning. It is by the examples of these values they personally offer their pupils that teachers demonstrate their centrality, and it is by the strategies and techniques they use in their lessons that they promote their pupils' growing possession of them.

CONCLUSION

Our starting point in this chapter was Standard 1.3 of *Qualifying to Teach*, and the indicative range of values, attitudes and behaviours that this Standard proposes teachers must *demonstrate* and *promote*. We have concentrated on what is involved in bringing these things to life in classrooms, and, in doing so, have

placed what the Standard requires within a much broader context suggested by other perspectives on effective teaching, on what makes for classrooms in which there is a healthy and positive climate for learning, and on work which is deliberately addressing pupils' own learning about learning. Underlying everything has been the view that a teacher needs not only to show that they possess and understand a range of essential professional characteristics which are founded on key pedagogical and professional values, but that they can plan, manage and achieve classroom practices which embody these values. It is by such practices that teachers can aim to achieve true transfer to learners of *both* knowledge *and* the essential values and attitudes which give that knowledge form, meaning and significance.

TASKS AND INVESTIGATIONS

Lesson observation: getting the whole picture

You will have opportunities to observe experienced teachers during the course of your teacher training programme, and may be encouraged in these lesson observations to concentrate on particular aspects of classroom management or pupils' learning. It is also valuable to look at lessons in the round, seeing how a whole lesson or teaching session is shaped in different phases.

For this task, tell the 'story' of a lesson you have observed following the model of 'A Lesson Observed' in this chapter. Your lesson might not fall into the same eight phases quite so clearly, but use the headings for those phases as a template for your own account:

> Meeting and greeting;
> Establishing routines;
> Mapping the lesson;
> Linking with previous learning;
> Encouraging responsibility for own learning;
> Building new learning;
> Promoting independence, initiative and engagement in learning; and
> Reinforcing, reviewing and conceptualising learning.

Use the bullet points concluding each phase in the example given in the chapter as prompts for particular things to look out for.

Complete the story of the lesson with a brief summary in 250–300 words highlighting the most significant classroom values which you identified in the lesson, and how you would seek to demonstrate them in your own practice.

Classroom climate

Choose one of the Hay McBer nine dimensions of Classroom Climate (in Research Perspective 2) and 'mind map' it (see Chapter 9), teasing out what you see as its key features and components in a class you are or will be teaching.

Empowering learners

Research Perspective 4 draws attention to the value of 'contexts that provide for choice and control' in developing students' achievement of self-regulation of thinking and learning processes. Consider – perhaps by debating it with one or two colleagues – the practical steps you can take to develop 'self-motivated learning' in your own work with students.

4 Expectations, Diversity and Achievement

It has often been said that schools 'cannot go it alone' against the forces of racial inequality, prejudice and social exclusion that are outside their gates but reach into the classroom. While that may be true, and offer some comfort to those schools who feel they are constantly battling against the odds, it must not become an excuse for failure to take action, because if schools do not take a stand, what hope is there for breaking the vicious circle of these corrosive forces which exist in society at large?

(OFSTED, 1999: 55)

The importance that the Department for Education Skills places upon educational inclusion is perhaps exemplified nowhere more clearly than in the OFSTED guidance for inspectors and schools *Evaluating Educational Inclusion* (OFSTED, 2000). The document begins by addressing inspectors in the following manner:

> **YOU MUST** pursue the following three questions which span the inspection schedule:
> **Do all pupils get a fair deal at school?**
> **How well does the school recognise and overcome barriers to learning?**
> **Do the school's values embrace inclusion and does its practice promote it?**
>
> **YOU MUST** focus your enquiries on significant groups of pupils who may not be benefiting enough from their education...
> **YOU MUST** evaluate and report on the effectiveness of the school in relation to these groups, as well as overall, in the relevant sections of the report...
> **YOU MUST** be familiar with all the evaluation criteria that relate to inclusion, the main provisions of equal opportunities and race relations law as they apply to schools and OFSTED's role in respect of the Macpherson Report. (p. 3) (*Emphasis in original document*)

It is, therefore, not surprising that the prime position in the list of *Professional Values and Practices* is given to a standard premised upon a belief in equality of educational opportunities. Standard 1.1 states that student teachers are expected to 'have high expectations of all pupils; respect their social, cultural, linguistic, religious and ethnic backgrounds; and are committed to raising their educational achievement'. The TTA *Handbook of Guidance* (TTA, 2003) is quite clear about the scope of the task involved in meeting this Standard, which encapsulates the essence of teaching and learning:

> Teachers need to know how to draw on their awareness and understanding of their pupils' social, cultural, linguistic, religious and ethnic backgrounds to support learning and to teach in ways that engage and challenge pupils.
>
> (TTA, 2003: 6)

In the early years of the twenty-first century the intrinsic truths of this statement might be thought to be self-evident. However, it might be argued that, for much of the past one hundred years the very opposite was the case in state schools. Clearly, it would be beyond the scope and space allowed to the current chapter to address the minutiae of knowledge, skills and understandings a student teacher needs to draw upon and develop in order to teach successfully in the rich racial, cultural and linguistic diversity that characterises many schools today. Instead this chapter will seek to explore some principles that have underpinned the development of teaching and learning in our schools and also consider those that might underpin an education based upon the transformative aspects of teaching and learning. Before considering issues relating to the educational attainment of pupils from minority ethnic groups, the first part of the chapter will focus upon issues related to class and gender, which in themselves, also permeate issues related to age, language, race, ethnicity, disability and religion. However, it is necessary to be mindful of the vital importance of developing an understanding of the issues related to, and a positive promotion of, equality of educational opportunities for pupils from *all* backgrounds, as this quotation from the OFSTED publication, *Educational Opportunity* (Gillborn and Mirza, 2000), reminds us:

> Equality of opportunity is a vital issue of social and economic importance to the whole of society. Traditionally, racial equality has been perceived as specialist area of only marginal significance in comparison with issues such as social class and gender, which, it is sometimes argued, affect everyone. This view which assumes that minority ethnic performance is only of relevance to the minorities themselves, is out of date in the context of the wider economic and social trends towards global diversity and the necessity for a sustainable multiculturalism. If any individual is denied the

opportunity to fulfil their potential because of their racial, ethnic, class or gender status it is now widely understood that society as a whole bears a social and economic cost by being deprived the fruits of their enterprise, energy and imagination.

The performance of all pupils from all backgrounds is of relevance to all teachers, headteachers, parents, employers and educational policy makers. It should be remembered that diversity itself is also diverse. The cohort of pupils in any school may be made up from children from a range of diverse 'groups'. These groups are not mutually exclusive and any one pupil might belong to a number of these groups simultaneously. The term 'group' is used here merely as an aid to discussion and should not be seen as describing a particular, discrete, homogenous collection of pupils. Such 'groups' then might be:

- girls;
- boys;
- pupils from minority ethnic backgrounds;
- pupils from particular faith communities;
- travellers;
- asylum seekers;
- refugees;
- working-class children;
- middle-class children;
- pupils with English as an Additional Language (EAL);
- pupils with special educational needs;
- gifted and talented pupils;
- disabled pupils;
- children in the care of the local authority; and
- any pupil at risk of disaffection and exclusion.

This list is by no means comprehensive as there are many other contextual factors that will have a bearing upon the teaching and learning of pupils in school. Hopefully, however, the list provides an idea of the range of the contexts in which pupils in class lead their lives. (For more information and a full consideration of the issues here, see Chapter 3 'Groups at Particular Risk' in Department for Education and Employment (DfEE) Circular 10/99 *Social Inclusion: Pupil Support*.) In a chapter of this length it would be impossible to consider in detail each of the groups listed above and to fully explore all the issues that face LEAs, schools, community groups, teachers, parents and pupils in relation to inclusion without the risk of trivialisation. Rather, the intention of this chapter is to consider key aspects of diversity and inclusion related to some groups as exemplifying the issues that need to be addressed in relation to all groups.

Shortly after the second statement quoted above, the *Handbook of Guidance* (TTA, 2003) contains the following caveat concerning teachers' roles in this regard: 'However, they should avoid making assumptions about their pupils' abilities or potential based upon their backgrounds.' The full import of this statement might not at first be apparent, but it reminds that far from being a statement of the obvious, for nearly one hundred years, state education was founded almost entirely upon such assumptions. Judgements about the educability and suitability of children to follow particular curricula was based not only upon the socio-cultural backgrounds of pupils, but also upon their sex.

SCHOOLING AND UNDERACHIEVEMENT

In the latter half of the twentieth century a variety of aspects of school life were examined in order to identify the causes of pupil underachievement: access, institutional structures, the nature of school knowledge to name but a few. It is well documented that, despite the intentions of Education Acts from 1944 to 1988, children from the working class have continued to underachieve at school. Floud *et al.* (1966) exposed massive underrepresentation of working-class boys at grammar schools. Douglas (1964) showed how working-class pupils with the same IQ scores as middle-class children were failing to gain grammar school places, because of the bias of teachers in primary schools. And the IQ tests themselves were shown to have a middle-class bias in their content. It is also now well known that the eleven-plus scores of girls were adjusted down because as a group they were far outstripping boys' achievement (see *The Report of the Task Group on Assessment and Testing (TGAT)* (DES, 1987: 40–53) for a discussion of these issues in relation to the establishment of the National Curriculum).

Hargreaves (1967), Lacey (1970) and Ball (1981) have cited the institutional structures of schools, such as streaming and banding, as influential in determining the performance of working-class pupils: a disproportionate number of whom were found to be represented in the lower streams and bands. For others, such as Brown (1973), Bourdieu (1973) and Bowles and Gintis (1976) it is the stratification of school knowledge that reproduces inequalities in 'cultural capital': the different values, beliefs and behaviours of an individual that are the product of socialisation from birth into a cultural group. This cultural inheritance can be translated into such social resources as status, power and wealth. There is a significant difference between the cultural capital of working-class and middle-class children. Children who are socialised into the dominant culture will have a big advantage over children not socialised into this culture as schooling attempts to reproduce dominant cultural values and ideas.

However, this is not to say that working-class pupils are simply passive recipients of a dominant culture, for studies by Gaskell (1985) and Willis (1977, 1981) for example, have shown how pupils resist school culture – although Abraham's (1993) study reveals that resistance comes more from 'anti-school' pupils whatever their social background. Abraham (1993: 136) goes on to argue that

> the organising and processing of school knowledge provides a setting which is not sufficiently critical of social class and gender divisions to discourage their reproduction in further schooling and out into the occupational structure.

The last decade of the twentieth century began with a Conservative prime minister announcing that society did not exist and drew to a close with a New Labour prime minister announcing that 'we' are now all members of the middle class. It has become unfashionable in recent years to discuss social class and education. There appears to be an underlying assumption that it is now passé to do so: the debate has moved on; social class is an irrelevance. Indeed, it could be argued that the issue has never been properly tackled. In the early 1980s the Inner London Education Authority (ILEA) launched its 'Sex, Race and Class' initiative. While the ILEA did much work relating to the first two, for all its egalitarian zeal, it shied away from grasping the nettle of class.

Government figures produced in 1991 showed that only five per cent of children from skilled manual home backgrounds attended university (Social Trends, 1992) and despite a claimed 30 per cent increase in access to university, in 1998 only approximately five per cent of those at university came from the poorest post-coded areas (Halsey, 1998). Despite the inception of the National Curriculum designed to ensure an equal curricular entitlement for all pupils, children from working-class backgrounds are underachieving. Statistics of the Organisation for Economic Cooperation and Development (OECD, 1997) declare eight million adults in the United Kingdom to be 'functionally illiterate'.

CURRICULUM DIFFERENTIATION

'Differentiation' in the classroom is a current term within educational discourse that has very positive connotations. It is associated with the construction and management of teaching and learning in ways that meet individual needs and interests in order that all pupils achieve their full potential. In the past, however, the term 'differentiated curriculum' had almost the opposite meaning. Chapter 7 *The Community and the School*, shows how curriculum construction and provision had been differentiated particularly along gender lines in order to meet the adult needs in the perceived future lives of pupils. For an account of the deliberate domestic orientation of curriculum subjects aimed at girls, see Kamm (1971: 42–46), Sharpe (1976: 14–15) and Burstyn (1980: 43–92).

In 1959 the Crowther Report considers it 'sound educational policy to take account of natural interests'. The *natural* interests of a girl are defined as 'dress, personal appearance and problems in human relations' because 'the incentive for girls to equip themselves for marriage and home-making is genetic'. Therefore, the Report proposes that such concerns 'should be a central part of her education' (Ministry of Education, 1959: 32). Clearly, the authors of the Report were not in agreement with John Stuart Mill, who had argued that 'calling distinctions in their social and intellectual situation 'Nature' is pre-eminently a political act' (1909: 27).

Four years later, the Newsom Report, *Half Our Future* (Ministry of Education, 1963) on the education of thirteen- to sixteen-year-old children 'of less than average ability', avers that girls 'may need all the more the education that a good school can give in the wider aspects of home-making, and in the skills that will reduce the element of domestic drudgery' (Ministry of Education, 1963: 135). However, it is aware of the dangers of an over emphasis on curriculum differentiation in relation to practical subjects. The Report states, 'We have not labelled crafts "boys" or "girls", although workshop crafts will be taken by boys and domestic crafts by girls…We welcome, however, the fact that some schools achieve sufficiently flexible organisation to allow boys to take cookery if they wish, and girls, handicraft or technical drawing; and where a school has vocationally-slanted courses related for example to catering or the clothing trades, the conventional divisions of boys' and girls' interests will clearly not apply' (1963: 131). These are fine sentiments, but on the following page, in its discussion of the 'vocational relevance' of art and related crafts, the Report states that, 'Design, function, decoration, display and communication, have special significance for those who may one day work in shops, in commerce, in the dress and clothing and furnishing trades, in textiles, buildings and printing; and, not least, for the future housewife' (Ministry of Education, 1963: 132).

The passing of the Sex Discrimination Act in 1975 made it illegal to discriminate directly or indirectly. In relation to schooling, direct discrimination would result if pupils were debarred from the study of a subject because of their sex, whereas indirect discrimination would result from the application of a condition or conditions that made it unlikely that either boys or girls could comply. The Central Office of Information (COI) published *Women in Britain* in 1975 and the data it contained showed a remarkable disparity between girls and boys in the entry for examinations in England and Scotland. In Home Economics 1,40,000 girls took the examination compared to 2,800 boys, while in Chemistry 85,000 girls were entered compared to 2,80,000 boys. At Advanced level, twice as many girls as boys were entered for Arts subjects, whereas in the Sciences and Mathematics, the proportion was reversed (COI, 1975: 9). In the same year *Education Survey 21* (DES, 1975) on curricular differences for boys and girls also contained data that showed just how deeply the lines of division extended on the basis of sex (1975: 25–9). The *Survey* proposed that:

Whatever differences that may continue ought to be based on genuine choice: choice openly offered to all who reveal the necessary interest, ability and determination, and not choice based on traditional assumptions about the 'proper' spheres of interest and influence of men and women.

(1975: 24)

One year after the Sex Discrimination Act had been passed, the Race Relations Act, 1976 became law. Section 17 of the Act makes discrimination in education unlawful. (See Chapter 9 for a discussion of the legal responsibilities of the teacher.)

ATTAINMENT OF PUPILS FROM MINORITY ETHNIC GROUPS

In 1996, OFSTED published *Recent Research on the Achievements of Ethnic Minority Pupils* (Gilborn and Gipps, 1996) and followed it by focusing a series of inspections of approximately 90 schools on 'the effectiveness of initiatives to raise the attainment of minority ethnic pupils, especially those from Bangladeshi, Black Caribbean, Pakistani and Gypsy Traveller backgrounds' (OFSTED, 1999).

The key questions that the inspections sought to answer were:

- What evidence do schools have on the relative performance of pupils from different ethnic groups?
- What strategies have schools implemented to raise the attainment of minority ethnic groups?
- What policies have schools developed for tackling stereotyping, ensuring high expectations and promoting good race relations?
- How do LEAs assist and work on partnership to achieve successful outcomes in these three areas?

The inspections found that although the attainment of pupils from minority ethnic groups as a whole is improving, some groups continue to underachieve. In particular in the early years of schooling, the performance of Bangladeshi and Pakistani pupils remains depressed. Nevertheless, once these pupils' proficiency in English improves, their attainment 'often matches or even surpasses that of first language English speaking pupils in similar circumstances' (OFSTED, 1999: 7). However, their generally lower attainment in the higher General Certificate of Secondary Education (GCSE) grades must remain a matter of concern. The Report also concluded that while Black Caribbean pupils start well in primary schools, their performance declines markedly in secondary school. The group found to be most at risk were Gypsy Traveller pupils whose 'generally low attainment is a matter of serious concern' (OFSTED, 1999: 7). While mindful of the complexities related to any perceived homogeneity of 'groups' noted earlier, *Raising the Attainment of Minority Ethnic Pupils* notes, 'In general, girls from minority ethnic groups attain more highly than boys' (OFSTED, 1999: 7).

The Report highlighted examples of successful practice that included the observation that schools in which pupils from minority ethnic groups flourish, clearly understood the hostility that these pupils often face (especially Gypsy Traveller children). Such schools had developed strategies for countering stereotyping that have had a 'tangible impact on pupils' self esteem' and that have influenced the attitudes of the majority of pupils. Similarly, an open and vigilant school ethos is a successful feature of successful race relations. Such an ethos is supported by structures that enable pupils to talk about their concerns and share in the development of strategies for their resolution (OFSTED, 1999: 8). The Report also concluded that in schools that had been most successful in raising the attainment of pupils from minority ethnic groups, headteachers and senior managers in these schools made it clear that the underperformance of any group of pupils was unacceptable. Furthermore, these senior managers gathered evidence regularly and systematically and challenged departments and individuals to give an account of how they intended to improve matters.

Nevertheless, while the Report also found that a majority of schools engaged in a range of initiatives to improve provision and raise the attainment of all pupils, few schools monitored these activities systematically. Additionally, it was rare that such activities had a specific ethnic focus. Similarly, while all schools had equal opportunities policies, few schools had clear procedures for monitoring their implementation. Consequently, the impact of policy on practice was limited. There is a danger that schools will establish working parties on particular issues and produce reports and policies that once published will sit on shelves. Teachers need to be mindful of the erroneous belief that once a policy has been written, the job is done. Clearly, this is not the case.

More widely, the Report also found that fewer than a quarter of LEAs visited had clear strategies for raising the attainment of pupils from minority ethnic groups. Ultimately, the Report concluded:

> Despite some pockets of sound practice this survey shows that many schools and LEAs are not nearly as effective as they should be in tackling the underachievement of minority ethnic groups.
>
> (OFSTED, 1999: 54)

Since 1999 there have been wide-ranging and significant changes related to the provision for the achievement of pupils from minority ethnic groups. Since 1999 schools have been required to set targets for achievement at the end of Key Stages 2 and 4, with the expectation that targets cover improved performance by pupils from minority ethnic groups. Since that time LEAs have been required to produce

Education Development Plans in which they set out the action that is planned to support school improvement, which is based upon an audit of the strengths and weaknesses of school performance, including the achievement of pupils from minority ethnic groups.

In April 1999 the Ethnic Minority Achievement Grant (EMAG) was introduced, which is designed to assist schools in their work to address underachievement and to help ensure that such work is anchored in mainstream improvement activity in the school. The grant replaced the education element of Home Office Section 11 funding. Worth £154 million in 2000–02, that element of the grant is administered by the DfES.

The publication, in February 1999, of the Macpherson Report (Stationery Office, 1999) on the inquiry into the murder of south London teenager Stephen Lawrence led to the passing of the Race Relations (Amendment) Act in 2000. The Act places a general duty on LEAs and schools to avoid discrimination on racial grounds and to promote good race relations. One year after the publication of the Act, in October 2001, OFSTED published *Managing Support for the Attainment of Pupils from Minority Ethnic Groups* (OFSTED, 2001) that evaluated developments in the work of LEAs and schools to promote higher achievement by pupils from minority ethnic groups and followed up the 1999 Report discussed above.

The opening of the *Main Findings* of the Report contains disappointing news for those who had been engaged in the developments of the preceding years: 'LEA support for the attainment of pupils from minority ethnic groups is still too variable'. However, the support is described as 'improving' (OFSTED, 2001: 3). It notes that planning of provision for pupils from minority ethnic groups contained in Education Development Plans is 'too often ineffective' (ibid.). However, the Report does identify the characteristics of effective LEA management of support for raising the attainment of pupils from minority ethnic groups. These are:

- clear delineation of responsibilities;
- genuine delegation of management responsibilities to schools;
- a clear understanding of shared principles;
- an acceptance by schools that support for raising the attainment of pupils from minority ethnic groups is integral to the pursuit of higher standards;
- the use of attainment data to identify needs;
- the allocation of funding and the deployment of staff to meet needs;
- competent specialist staff, with effective arrangements for supporting their development;
- contingency funding to cope with unpredictable influxes of pupils; and
- detailed joint planning at the LEA and school level.

(OFSTED, 2001: 3)

As a result of the School Standards and Framework Act (1998), LEAs are required to set out how they propose to discharge their functions with a view to promoting higher standards in schools. The Report describes the characteristic features of the most informative Education Development Plans. They include:

- data on the ethnic composition of the whole population of an area, together with information describing the distribution of minority ethnic groups across the LEA's schools;
- data by ethnicity and gender describing the performance of pupils from the major minority groups, including baseline data as well as performance at the four Key Stages and post-16;
- data by ethnicity and gender on other matters including exclusions, attendance, mobility and post-16 destinations;
- data on the language proficiency of pupils learning EAL;
- detailed commentary that draws attention to particular issues needing action;
- signs of a clear intent to address issues which are important matters of principle, even though they may affect relatively few individuals – for example, strategies to support children experiencing racial harassment;
- targets for improved performance and participation by minority ethnic groups;
- careful specification of the way support for pupils from minority ethnic groups is to be integrated within the programmes planned to address overall LEA priorities;
- specification of the staffing devoted to support minority ethnic achievement, including funding sources, and a clear indication of how the roles of the staff involved link with those of mainstream advisers;
- a statement of the training needs of a range of staff as judged by the LEA, and what its training programme will offer; and
- arrangements for the quality assurance of EMAG-funded and other support for minority ethnic achievement.

(OFSTED, 2001: 13)

Once again, it is clear that detailed and careful proactive management is one of the key contributors to a successful approach to the raising of attainment of pupils from minority ethnic groups. Among the *Conclusions* of the Report are the following observations: 'The trend in LEA inspection reports gives some grounds for optimism that LEAs' work in relation to minority ethnic achievement is improving.... There is, however, still some way to go...'(OFSTED, 2001: 39). The Report also notes earlier that 'There is, of course, only so much that LEAs can do... raising attainment depends on good management and teaching in schools' (OFSTED, 2001: 10). *Managing Support for the Attainment of Pupils from Minority Ethnic Groups* is not dodging the issue here, rather it is clearly identifying that as well as LEAs, inspectors, headteachers and senior managers, it is the duty of each experienced teacher, Newly Qualified Teacher, and indeed student teacher, to develop knowledge, understanding, skills and practices that will ensure that their classrooms are models of inclusive pedagogy.

INCLUSION

OFSTED inspectors ask the following questions to test educational inclusivity:

- Are all pupils achieving as much as they can, and deriving the maximum benefit, according to their individual needs, from what the school provides?
- If not, which pupils or groups of pupils are not achieving as much as they can? Why not?
- Is the school aware of these differences? If not, why not?
- How does the school explain differences between groups of pupils in terms of achievement, teaching and learning and access to curricular opportunities? Are these explanations well founded and convincing?
- What action (including use of nationally funded or local initiatives) has the school taken or is it taking to raise the standards of attainment of pupils or groups of pupils who appear to be underachieving or at particular risk? If none, why?
- If the school is taking action, is it appropriate and is it effective or likely to be effective?
- Are there any unintended consequences? How well are these consequences being handled?
- What action is being taken by the school to promote racial harmony, to prepare pupils for living in a diverse and increasingly interdependent society and specifically to prevent and address racism, sexism and other forms of discrimination?

(OFSTED, 2000: 6)

The *Index for Inclusion* (CSIE, 2000) is a set of materials produced as a result of a three-year collaborative project between the Centre for Studies on Inclusive Education, the Centre for Educational Needs, Manchester University, the Centre for Educational Research, Canterbury Christ Church College and a number of Local Education Authorities including Birmingham, Tower Hamlets, Harrow and Stockport. The purpose of the pack is to support schools in a process of inclusive school development by drawing on the views of governors, teachers and other staff, parents and carers, pupils and other community members.

The *Index* process comprises five phases of collaborative work: Starting the *Index* process; Finding out about the school; Producing an inclusive School Development Plan; Implementing developments; and Reviewing the *Index* process. The process is cyclical in nature with the fifth phase looping back into the second in order that the process is recursive and developmental. The process has the hallmarks of effective practice highlighted by successive OFSTED inspections: careful and thorough planning. However, the process goes further:

> The *Index* is not only about a carefully planned, step-by-step process of change as assumed in many approaches to school development planning. The *Index* is also concerned with changes in cultures and values which may enable staff and students to adopt inclusive practices which go beyond any particular identified priority.
>
> (CSIE, 2000)

The power of the *Index* lies in its three interconnected *dimensions* (CSIE, 2000: 10) of school life:

Dimension A: Creating inclusive cultures

1   Building community
2   Establishing inclusive values

Dimension B: Producing inclusive policies

1   Developing a school for all
2   Organising support for diversity

Dimension C: Evolving inclusive practices

1   Orchestrating learning
2   Mobilising resources

The strength of this approach to the development of educational inclusivity is that it is structured and carefully planned, but above all the process is in itself inclusive by involving the participation in the process of all members of the school's community (CSIE, 2000: 12). In itself, the *Index* is a model of excellent practice designed to contribute to the development of excellent practice in school.

MEETING THE STANDARD

It might appear that the first Standard in the list of *Professional Values and Practices* is the most far reaching and ultimately the most daunting. Indeed, it underpins every aspect of the role of the teacher and goes to the very heart of educational practice in schools today. Additionally, the TTA *Handbook of Guidance* notes that evidence for meeting Standard 1.1 will also be drawn from a student teacher's work in relation to Standard 3.1.1 – valuing diversity and setting high expectations; Standard 3.3.6 – taking account of varying backgrounds; or Standard 3.3.14 – responding effectively to equal opportunities issues.

Chapter 8 discusses reflective practice and commitment to professional development and comments on the multiplicity of skills, knowledge, understandings and life experiences that student teachers bring to their courses. Every cohort of beginning teachers will itself be diverse. It may be quite daunting to find that you are placed in a school with children from diverse racial, ethnic and class backgrounds many of which are entirely different from your own. How is it possible in an already packed teacher education course to find the time and space to become expert upon a diverse range of cultures?

However, it is important to be very clear about the scope of this Standard and the expectations held by those charged with the assessment of student teachers against it. The TTA *Handbook of Guidance* is quite clear on this matter:

> This Standard is about trainee teachers' *attitudes* and *professional relationships* with their pupils. It does not imply the need for comprehensive knowledge of the backgrounds of the pupils they teach.
>
> (2003: 6 our italics)

The *Handbook* goes on to say that evidence of student teachers' commitment, attitudes, behaviour and expectations of pupil achievement are likely to emerge in 'every aspect of their work'. Certainly, attitudes and professional commitment will be quite evident in any observations of lessons, but also judgements will be made on evidence drawn from planning and evaluation of lessons (see also Chapter 8):

- How has the trainee used evidence of past achievement to set challenging teaching and learning objectives for all pupils?
- Is the trainee aware of the issues that are likely to be faced by pupils from a variety of backgrounds?
- Does the trainee select resources and materials that show they value diversity and are sensitive to the needs of different groups?

Of particular interest is another TTA publication *Raising the Attainment of Minority ethnic Pupils: Guidance and resource materials for providers of initial teacher training* (TTA, 2000). This is an excellent ring binder of materials that your provider will have. Indeed, there are likely to be copies of it in your library.

The main focus of this guidance is on preparing trainee teachers to understand and meet the educational needs of pupils from minority ethnic groups. 'However, the guidance should be seen in the wider context of a concern for social justice for all, and the principles underlying it as more widely applicable and having implications for promoting the educational inclusion of other groups and for the education of all pupils' (TTA, 2000: 9). The intention of the guidance is to help trainees to:

- understand how inequality operates structurally, institutionally and culturally as well as at a personal level;
- understand the main issues relating to the differential performance in schooling of some groups of minority ethnic pupils;
- know some of the ways in which successful teachers and schools work to raise pupil attainment and the quality of their education and prepare pupils to live in a socially just, democratic, pluralist society;
- know how to employ in their own practice, strategies that are effective in raising the attainment of minority ethnic pupils and which improve the quality of their education; and
- know where to go to find additional information and support.

(TTA, 2000: 10)

Raising the Attainment of Minority Ethnic Pupils: Guidance and resource materials for providers of initial teacher training is a thorough and extensive resource that comprises eleven sections, which include *inter alia* 'Including all pupils, setting the context', 'An inclusive curriculum', 'Understanding social, cultural and religious issues', 'The Early Years', 'Teaching refugee pupils' and 'Effective links between the school and the wider community'. Although each of its eleven sections is related in detail to the previous set of teacher training Standards from Circular 4/98, the document shows clearly how inclusive practice underpins all areas of teaching and learning and it is a valuable resource that will develop your knowledge, understandings and skills.

The final aim of the Guidance is perhaps the most important. Its purpose is to:

- develop critical attitudes in dealing with information and assumptions about minority ethnic groups.

(TTA, 2000: 10)

Ultimately teachers that meet Standard 1.1 will actively seek to find out about their pupils and use that knowledge positively in order to enable all pupils from all backgrounds to make progress in their learning. The ultimate goal will always be to raise the achievement of all pupils whatever the context.

Although writing for science teachers, Turner and Turner (1994) provide excellent guidance for student teachers in this area that includes many of the following activities. Although it may be obvious from the first moment you walk into your placement school, you should be aware that you are teaching pupils to live in a culturally diverse society. In order to develop your own understandings and awareness you will need to find out about the main cultural groups in your school – for example, the practices of particular faith groups, what the cultural norms and expectations are, how many different home languages there are. You should work to develop the knowledge to be able to recognise the different cultural groups in your classes. You should also prepare appropriate resources, materials and displays for your teaching subject that are not ethnocentric, which, nevertheless, you should also monitor for bias and stereotyping.

In order to fully understand a school's mission in this regard, you should seek out school/LEA policy documents and develop a good working knowledge of the main features of the school's equal opportunities policies on race, multiculturalism, gender, class, disability and, indeed, on bullying. In your classroom and in your daily involvement in the corporate life of the school (see Chapter 7) promote respect and understanding between all groups in the school including boys and girls, men and women.

You will need to prepare lessons that recognise the gender balance in your class and to teach in a manner that is aware of gender issues in relation to classroom interactions. Similarly, you should seek to prepare and teach lessons that recognise and celebrate the racial and cultural diversity in your class. You will need to be sensitive to the opportunities to oppose sexism and racism in the classroom and around the school. It is also most important that you actively endeavour to diminish bias and stereotyping in the classroom by monitoring the classroom interactions of both pupils and teachers. For example, what messages are conveyed by teachers who, when calling for attention in a mixed class, address male pupils as 'Chaps' or 'Guys' or 'Gentlemen' and female pupils as 'Girls'?

Language is central to teaching and learning. Therefore, you should develop and show in your classroom practice an understanding of the importance of language in teaching and learning – both written and spoken. Likewise, show this understanding in your lesson preparation, planning and evaluation. It will also be of help to develop a secure knowledge of those pupils who are bilingual (and also multilingual) in your class and those who are receiving, or who need, EAL support. You should also develop a good knowledge of those pupils who have special educational needs in your classroom, whether they be pupils who experience particular learning or behavioural difficulties, or those who are regarded as gifted and talented. It goes without saying that your planning, preparation, teaching and evaluation of your lessons will be sensitive to the needs and interests of all these pupils. Capel *et al.* (2003) from whom some of the foregoing has been adapted, provide excellent support on issues related to 'Pupil Differences'.

CONCLUSION

In September 2003, the TTA supported the development of a Professional Resource Network on Diversity based at London Metropolitan University. The aim of this network is to enable student teachers better to raise the achievement of pupils from diverse backgrounds. Over three years *Multiverse*, as the project is known, will develop networks of experienced teacher educators, LEAs, schools and community groups; organise seminars and conferences focused upon key issues and create an electronic resource bank of resources and materials for all those engaged in teacher education. Student teachers, teachers, mentors, tutors, LEA advisors, educational consultants, academics and educational policy makers will be able to contribute to the 'Resource Bank, Exchange and Forum' via the *Multiverse* website: www.multiverse.ac.uk.

Meeting this Standard requires you to build on and to extend your knowledge and understanding about the contexts in which you will be learning to teach and the range of communities, cultures and sub-cultures in the area served by your school. Throughout your career, you will be expected to promote and implement policies and practices that encourage mutual tolerance and respect for diversity that challenge discrimination. The skills, beliefs, attitudes and values you display in the classroom and in your wider contribution to the life of the school, will be informed by and reflected in your approach to contexts in which you are working. It is an old adage that the pessimist sees the glass half empty, while the optimist sees it half full. Ultimately, perhaps, your approach to this Standard might be seen in your celebrating the richness of, and the possibilities offered by, the linguistic and cultural diversity in your schools. While you should accept and acknowledge the challenges and demands of teaching diverse groups of pupils, you should emphasise the positives rather than regarding diversity as a problem.

TASK   Key questions

In order to gain a full picture of your school's approach to raising the achievement of pupils from diverse groups, draw upon the key OFSTED questions quoted under the section 'Inclusion'. Find answers to the following:

- What evidence does your school have on the relative performance of pupils from different minority ethnic and other groups listed in this chapter?
- What strategies has the school implemented to raise the attainment of pupils from minority ethnic and other groups?
- What policies has the school developed for tackling stereotyping, ensuring high expectations and promoting good race relations? How do these policies translate into practice in the classroom?
- How does the LEA assist and work on partnership to achieve successful outcomes in these three areas?

5 Professional Relations with Parents and Pupils

Pupils are more likely to learn if they recognise that their teachers value them as individuals and respond to them consistently. Pupils are more likely to treat others with respect and consideration if their teachers demonstrate such behaviour towards them.

(TTA, 2003: 4)

...We have built a parents suite at the centre of the school near the head's office and staff rooms...This is the first step in a philosophy which places parents at the centre as the prime educators. Why are parents so important? Teachers may have contact with young people for 30 hours a week. But parents have the longer-term involvement: parents are the prime educators. Teachers have a commitment to a young person over a period of time which then terminates: parents have the longer-term commitment...There must, therefore, be the possibility of parents and teachers working together co-operatively and collaboratively to educate the child. Parents should have access to the education process as a right...I don't believe in a parental veto. But we need a partnership between parents and teachers. Sometimes the school needs to act as the advocate of the child: we cannot always assume that the wants of the parents correspond to the child's needs. They don't always.

A Headteacher (in Nixon *et al.*, 1996: 109)

Chapters 1 and 2 discussed how teachers need constantly to clarify and review their own values and attitudes as it is these values and attitudes that will contribute significantly to who we are: they will underpin our professional identity. In preparing to teach you will need to consider what the expectations of the children you teach are and adopt a broader perspective in your teaching that takes account of the fact that you are preparing children for a life after school as responsible citizens. Those awarded QTS will inevitably need to demonstrate that they 'can communicate sensitively and effectively with parents and carers, recognising their role in pupils' learning, and their rights, responsibilities and interests in this'. They will also need to demonstrate that 'they treat pupils consistently, with respect and consideration'. In these two sections of the Standards (Sections 1.4 and 1.2) teachers, both new and experienced, are required to respect parents and pupils and show consideration to them as partners in the teaching and learning process. Chapters 6 and 9 cover the context of wider professional relations by the teacher. Parental involvement in schools and the kinds of care and respect provided for pupils will vary depending on the school you find yourself in during teaching practice or in your first teaching appointment. Practice in both these areas will vary considerably from school to school as each school generally develops its own way of involving parents and caring for its pupils – there is no standard practice. It is interesting that chapters dealing with these two areas (of teachers as role models and parental involvement in schools) are often absent from the various books which offer guidance to students during their teaching practice. These areas can certainly be complex and challenging for the new teacher. Matters are made more complex by virtue of the fact that there is no one standard by which one can determine what represents good practice from school to school. This complexity is best illustrated by a consideration of the principle expressed by the Latin tag, *in loco parentis*.

TEACHERS *IN LOCO PARENTIS*

The principle of *in loco parentis* was first outlined in the case of *Fitzgerald* v. *Northcote* in 1865. It states that when a parent places their child with a teacher they delegate to him/her all their own authority, so far as it is necessary for the welfare of the child. More recently *in loco parentis* has developed to mean the teacher acting as a prudent parent. Teachers have therefore been judged in the courts on the standard of the prudent parent. Section 2(9) of The Children Act 1989 states that: 'A person who has parental responsibility for a child may not surrender or transfer any part of that responsibility to another but may arrange for some or all of it to be met by one or more persons acting on his behalf.' In the light of this, schools need to establish before a child is admitted to a school the answer to the question: Who has parental responsibility for this child? This is essential due to the increasing prevalence of less-traditional parenting structures in society and the use of the term 'parents' in this chapter refers to home carers and guardians as well as natural parents.

In regard to the position of the teacher, Section 3(5) of the Act states: 'A person who –

(a)   does not have parental responsibility for a particular child, but
(b)   has care of the child – may (subject to the provisions of the Act) do what is reasonable in all the circumstances of the care for the purpose of safeguarding or promoting the child's welfare'.

Clearly the teacher owes a statutory duty of care towards the child in his or her class but some have questioned the usefulness of the principle of *in loco parentis*, especially as a teacher may well be responsible for over thirty children at one time (Hyams, 1997). Teachers who deliver a National Curriculum and are judged fit for teaching according to national standards of competence may also be seen as servants of the State as opposed to being viewed as standing in for the parent.

The teacher of infant-aged children for example will be expected to demonstrate the way they utilise their teaching ability and skills to create a sense of security in class. They will protect the children in their care and promote qualities of self-esteem and confidence. They will show the children that they are valued and loved. In this situation, they inevitably share in parental responsibility and might be said to be truly acting *in loco parentis*. Home visiting by infant teachers is also common and leads to greater contact with parents and the sharing of information.

In contrast, the sixth-form teacher who teaches a particular subject to examination level does not have to demonstrate all these qualities, but nevertheless does have a duty of care. The principle of *in loco parentis* in its strict sense, may not mean a great deal in the context of a sixth form. However, the teacher in any context must supervise his or her pupils/students and care for their health and safety. In summary, the Children Act defines parents as all those who have 'parental responsibility' for a child whether or not they are a natural parent. New teachers need to remember that they will be expected to 'do what is reasonable in all the circumstances of the care for the purpose of safeguarding or promoting the child's welfare' – they have a duty of care. Consequently, every teacher needs to take reasonable steps to avoid exposing the child to any dangers that are reasonably foreseeable.

A question which inevitably springs from a discussion of the duties of teachers is one of assessing the correlative rights of their students, of children in their class. The notion of 'right' is a complex one. In discussing the term, it is important to remember that its meaning can vary according to the context in which it is used. It should be borne in mind, that 'right' is used as shorthand in the following passages for a number of different species of legal entitlement. The United Nations Convention on the Rights of the Child and the European Convention on Human Rights (ECHR) would appear to be significant in any assessment of whether or not the notion of a right can attach to the child in the school. One practical result of the European jurisprudence in this area was the abolition of corporal punishment in State schools.

Another significant development in the sphere of rights, though not directly connected to the implementation of the European Convention in UK legislation was the production of a Parents Charter in 1991 (updated in 1994) by the DfES which gave greater emphasis to the role and rights of parents in regard to schools. The most fundamental right is of course the right to an education. This is not a right conferred by the ECHR and is interpreted as an economic and social right, having an aspirational, not an enforceable quality. Whilst there is much talk of rights, in reality children do not possess many rights. Pupils have no right to see their personal file or to challenge what others say or write about them unless it is clearly defamatory. They cannot appeal themselves against their suspension or exclusion from school nor can they control their participation in religious worship or the curriculum that is offered them. Children can also be detained by a school at the end of the school day without parental consent so long as the headteacher has given the parent 24-hour written notice of such detention. On the other hand, children can make a complaint against a teacher or member of staff. Whilst their rights in schools are extremely limited, their duties, whilst not legal, are large and cover anything from doing their homework to obeying school rules. The recognition of children's (as opposed to parental) rights in education in English domestic legislation is negligible, for the interests or rights of the child are subsumed by those of the parent. Some would argue that children should not be passive recipients of other people's decisions about what is in their best interests but rather should be active partners in determining what should happen to them.

The recent introduction of citizenship education that seeks to develop children as active citizens would also lend some support for this view. It is interesting here to briefly mention the Victoria Gillick case (1992) in which the House of Lords established the principle that a child of 'sufficient understanding and intelligence' has the power to give consent to medical treatment in their own right without the need for parental permission. It follows that the law has established a right to their confidentiality in medical matters being respected by, amongst other institutions, the school. This has presented difficult ethical problems for schools when children require time away from lessons for treatment from a doctor and explicitly demand that their parents not be informed. The law gives the right to a fourteen year old to take the 'morning after pill' without the knowledge of her parents, yet, quite possibly with the knowledge of a teacher (although this assumes that the child has volunteered the information as the teacher has no right to know the specific reasons why a child would be attending the doctor's in the first place). This again raises serious questions about what *in loco parentis* means for the teacher and when does the well-being of the child override any duty of confidentiality. It is true that the teacher cannot always give an undertaking that everything that is said in a conversation between him or her and a child will remain confidential. In addition, in law, there is no absolute recognition of confidentiality in the pupil /teacher relationship. The Gillick case could be interpreted as representing the recognition of a developing autonomy in teenagers.

Because teachers hold a position of trust and confidence with respect to children, high standards of conduct are expected of them at all times. Schooling is, in large part, about human relationships and teachers need to act as role models of responsible adult behaviour, attitudes and values. The teacher sets the tone for the modes of interaction in their class; their personality and values will reflect how life in the classroom is lived. According to Standard 1.2, new teachers must value their pupils as individuals and must be fair in dealings with them. They need to avoid causing their pupils embarrassment and attempt at all times to be constructive in their criticism and avoid showing favouritism. The teacher's respect for his or her pupils will inevitably involve genuine concern for them as human beings. The role of the teacher has been expressed in many terms. These include: mentor, guide and role model but whatever the term used the key feature of a teacher is that he or she helps form human beings. The teacher needs to be seen to be honest and be a person worthy of trust because he or she is the central moral authority in the classroom. This ethical positioning gives the teacher the right to tell children to follow directions, do their work, obey the school rules and end any behaviour that he or she considers to be contrary to the best interests of the child or group. In exercising this authority the teacher should not be authoritarian in approach, but act from his or her inner authority which should be infused with respect for children. It is why any form of discrimination by the teacher has no place in the school. Legislation such as the Sex Discrimination Act (1975), Race Relations Act (1976) and the Disability Discrimination Act (1995) make it unlawful to discriminate against a person on the grounds of sex, race or disability.

The Sexual Offences Act (2000) makes it a criminal offence if a teacher begins a relationship of a sexual nature with a child under the age of 18. The offence can carry a custodial sentence and will inevitably place the teacher on List 99 of the DfES which holds the names of all those people who have been prohibited from working with children and young people. New teachers should be aware of any child protection policies the school has but, in particular, new teachers should be aware of Circular 10/95 of the DfES on Protecting Children from Abuse which provides detailed guidance about physical contact with children and students. There are two paragraphs from this circular that are worth quoting in full here:

> It is unnecessary and unrealistic to suggest that teachers should touch pupils only in emergencies. Particularly with younger pupils, touching them is inevitable and can give welcome reassurance to the child. However, teachers must bear in mind that even perfectly innocent actions can sometimes be misconstrued. Children may find being touched uncomfortable or distressing for a variety of reasons. It is important for teachers to be sensitive to a child's reaction to physical contact and to act appropriately. It is also important not to touch pupils, however casually in ways or in parts of the body that might be considered indecent.
>
> Employers and senior staff have a responsibility to ensure that professional behaviour applies to relationships between staff and pupils or students, that all staff are clear about what constitutes appropriate behaviour and professional boundaries, and that those boundaries are maintained with the sensitive support and supervision required. That is

important in all schools, but residential institutions need to be particularly mindful of this responsibility as do individuals in circumstances where there is one to one contact with pupils, for example, in the teaching of music or extra curricular activities.

Teachers therefore have a duty to treat children appropriately in this regard and to ensure that when they are unsure of any aspect of their own teaching conditions with children then, clearly, advice should be sought from an appropriate colleague.

INSPECTIONS

Teachers are inspected in many value areas by OFSTED inspectors according to the Framework of Inspecting Schools (2003). The inspection criteria are presented as statements of good practice under different question headings. In Section 3.2 of the Framework, inspectors have to make judgements about the attitudes, behaviour and values fostered by the school. Inspectors look for ways in which teachers are actively cultivating the personal development of the pupils. For example, inspectors will assess the extent to which the pupils:

- show interest in school life and the range of activities provided;
- behave well in lessons and about the school;
- are enterprising and willing to take responsibility;
- are free from bullying, racism and other forms of harassment;
- form constructive relationships with others; and
- have confidence and self-esteem.

And they assess the extent to which the school:

- stimulates in pupils a desire for learning;
- sets high expectations of pupils' conduct and successfully implements policies to achieve them;
- promotes good relationships, including racial harmony; and
- deals effectively with incidents such as bullying, racism and other forms of harassment.

In addition to these, a range of other personal areas are covered by inspectors including whether pupils:

- understand and respect other people's feelings, values and beliefs;
- understand and apply principles that distinguish right from wrong; and
- understand and fulfil the responsibility of living in a community.

Teachers have a formative influence on the children they t
that they have good relations and are able effectively to
who have parental responsibility for the children they te

THE EDUCATIONAL RIGHTS OF PARENTS

Teachers and parents have a shared sense of purpose and share information about a child's development. This exchange of information between teacher and parent can aid effective and beneficial discourse with the school regarding the child. However, the involvement of parents in the school education of their children can be peripheral if it is restricted to activities such as fund – raising. Some schools seek to limit parental involvement to some specific tasks that are controlled by the school. Some home–school agreements that parents are asked to sign are an example of this type of cosmetic empowerment. It is not uncommon to hear teachers complain about the lack of parental support and to hear parents complain about the lack of information from school. But parent–teacher relations can be a genuine partnership. Parental involvement will largely depend on the school's attitude towards the concept. It can range from infrequent contacts with parents that are formalised and impersonal, to warm relations that are represented by mutual respect in which parents freely enter the school and classrooms. You, as a new teacher, will need to recognise that parents are already involved in the education of their child since parents are the first and foremost educators of their children. Parents have an essential but not exclusive right to educate their children. The choice of school is considered by many to be a fundamental right of every parent to ensure that the child is educated in accordance with the beliefs, values and religious principles of the family. It is also why there is an increasing emphasis on the rights of parents in education, a factor of which many parents have become aware. Legislation over the last twenty years in England has gradually provided parents with the following rights:

(a)   the right to choose a school for their child;
(b)   the right to appeal against a rejection of their child in the admissions process of a school;
(c)   the right of access to their child's records;
(d)   the right to have their confidentiality respected by the school;
(e)   the right to representation on a governing body;
(f)   the right to inspect the minutes of the governing body;
(g)   the right to establish a parents association;
(h)   the right to a meeting with the governing body at least once a year;
(i)   the right to receive copies of annual reports on the operation and performance of the school;

(j)   the right to appeal to the governing body against a decision to suspend or exclude their child from school;

(k)   the right to be consulted in relation to the assessment of the psychological or special needs of their child;

(l)   the right to a meeting in school to discuss the progress of their child; and

(m)   the right to withdraw their child from any form of religious worship.

Once again, it is important to bear in mind that the term 'right' does not mean the same in each example given above. They may fall into different legal categories. Some of these 'rights' are difficult to exercise by parents. In the context of 'rights talk' within education, there is a debate about whether or not parents are to be regarded as consumers, or whether they are partners in a relationship of equals. It is certainly the case that working with parents is often more talked about than practised. The Warnock Report in 1978 stated that 'Parents can be effective partners only if professionals take notice of what they say and how they express their needs, and treat their contributions as intrinsically important.' The new teacher needs to recognise the many different forms of right that parents have and devise ways in which they can co-operate with parents in the education of their children, always remaining within the framework policies of the school.

As you learn how to communicate more effectively with parents you will recognise and appreciate the important rights and role that parents have in the education of their children. Parents on the whole, are concerned with their child's welfare and will seek to act in the child's best interests. What the parent says must be treated with great seriousness; both the teacher and parent need to seek a shared purpose and develop mutual respect. You need to ensure that you make time to see parents and to respect any insights about the child that parents may offer. Parents can also support the school's policies on homework and in some cases may even directly support their own children in curriculum areas. Schools often interview parents before their child is admitted and on such occasions the aims of the school, the discipline and behaviour code are explained. Parents may be asked to sign an agreement that they have understood the code and accept joint responsibility for its implementation. In this 'contractual' way schools and parents become partners in accountability. Parents know that the teacher is a person who has a profound effect on the quality of education that their child experiences.

This idea of 'partnership' has long been recognised as a vital determinant of educational performance as well as a major factor in ensuring positive pupil behaviour, but the term is open to diverse interpretation. Research indicates that good communications between teachers and parents leads to higher expectations of pupils, better attendance in school and improved study habits. It is not surprising that successive governments, commissions and educational researchers have sought to increase the positive effects of this partnership between parents and teachers and between pupils and teachers. A 'partnership' of this nature will present challenges to the new teacher. Inexperienced teachers want to know how to develop professional relationships with parents and pupils and how to assist parents to share in the school-based education of their children. New teachers need to work alongside their more experienced colleagues in developing their writing and verbal skills in communicating with parents.

Good schools keep parents well informed of their children's progress both academically and 'morally, spiritually and socially'. Parents are legally entitled to a range of information from schools. This is done through newsletters, written reports on individual pupils, parental access to school records, meetings in school between parents and teachers as well as through parent–teacher associations. Keeping parents informed of a child's progress will be something that a new teacher will do in the daily marking of a child's work and in writing end-of-term reports. It is useful to consider what information parents want about their child. Broadfoot's research in this area (1989) lists the kinds of comments parents wanted from teachers:

- achievement orientated;
- factual;
- positive;
- broadly based;
- free of speculation and able to be substantiated;
- significant;
- related to learning goals;
- succinct; and
- constructive.

Parents also want to know that their child is happy in school. It is important to note here that teachers are covered by 'qualified privilege' when writing reports. This means that they cannot be sued for libel for writing negative comments about a child, unless it can be proved that they acted maliciously. Nevertheless, it is essential that new teachers follow precisely the standard practices of the school in relation to communications with parents and in particular that they avoid writing personal letters to parents without the explicit approval of the headteacher. Writing reports on children will include an assessment of aspects of their character as well as their academic ability so it is important that student teachers are prudent in their use of language. When speaking or writing to parents, the teacher should state their concerns about the child constructively, even when the ultimate message contains elements of negativity. Your aim should be to get a positive response from the parent. Broadfoot's list is a very good guide to follow for the new teacher in the absence of more detailed guidance from the school.

Parents often want factual information about their child, free of speculation or bias so new teachers need to learn the appropriate communication skills for this context. These skills might include:

> Listening;
> Knowing when to stop talking;
> Not interrupting parents when they are speaking;
> Not blaming parents for any difficulties;
> Not labelling parents;
> Giving advice sensitively;
> Showing interest in the child; and
> Being patient and polite.

Meeting parents face to face will be another area that new teachers will experience early in their career. Teachers should agree an agenda with parents in advance of any meetings and record any outcomes. It is the teacher's role to encourage not only co-operation from the parents, but also their participation. In summary, new teachers need to know the statutory rights of parents, particularly in terms of charting the progress of the child. They also need to know the importance of liaising with parents and have an understanding of their home circumstances. These home circumstances will raise issues of diversity and different styles of parenting. It is important that the teacher focuses on the involvement and inclusion of parents. Parents are sometimes not confident in dealing with teachers and can be unsure of themselves. This may be particularly true of some parents from ethnic minority groups who may not be able to articulate their concerns effectively. In these cases, an attitude of cultural diversity should be demonstrated by the teacher. Many parents, whatever their racial or socio-economic background, are anxious about dealing with teachers. Many parents believe that the teacher has omnipotent authority in the field of education. There is also the fact that some parents are very much involved in school activities whilst others are only seen when there is a problem to report about their child. These situations will require the teacher to be sensitive and understanding. Above all every parent should always be treated with courtesy and respect. Whilst this may sound onerous, Standard 1.4 does not expect student teachers to take sole responsibility for any of the school's communications in this area. Under the guidance of experienced teachers, student teachers need to demonstrate that they can contribute to draft reports and are able to shadow experienced staff at parents evenings.

It is useful for new teachers to be aware of Section 7 of OFSTED Framework for Inspection (2003) that deals with how well the school works in partnership with parents. Inspectors have to assess the extent to which:

- all parents are provided with relevant information about the school, and particularly about pupils' standards and progress;
- the school regularly seeks, values and acts on parents' views;
- the partnership with parents contributes to pupils' learning at school and at home; and
- the school does all it can to ensure satisfaction, and deals effectively with any concerns and complaints.

The school's teachers are inspected on how well as a community they develop effective working partnerships with parents. It would be useful for new teachers to look at the model of parent–teacher relations advocated by Chrispeels (1996) entitled 'Effective Schools and Home-School Partnership Roles: A Framework for Parental Involvement'. This model views parents as co-decision-makers with teachers in the education of their children.

TASKS

Statements of Values

Study the National Forum of Education and the Community's Statement of Values contained in the National Curriculum documentation. Do you agree with the statement? Which parts of the statement do you feel would be the most difficult to use or implement in your school? Which parts are already being implemented?

Values information on schools

Collect the following information in your teaching file:

- Collate all the standard letters that your school sends to parents into your teaching file;
- Seek out a copy of the school's policy on home–school links;
- Does the school have a statement on child-protection policy?
- List the times in the year when parents are invited formally into the school e.g. parents evenings, open days, school events, etc.; and
- Does your school have a home–school agreement that is signed by parents and the headteacher? Find out what the legal status is of this document. What are the contents of this document in terms of what is being agreed by the parent and the school?

Inspection of values

You should consult two OFSTED school reports on schools in the area in which you are teaching. Read Sections 3.2 and 7 and list the areas where the inspectors feel the schools have strengths and where they feel the schools have areas that might be improved. Compile a short table of your findings and then discuss these with your school mentor in relation to your own school.

CONCLUSION

In a democracy, parents do not have absolute legal authority over their children as the child has a number of rights. Within the context of schooling, children as pupils only have limited rights, and these are not all of the same category or easily defined. Nonetheless, parents are the first educators of the child and seek to nurture them to a point where they can act and decide for themselves. Teachers are given the task of caring for their children in such a way that they cultivate the values, attitudes and beliefs that parents desire to see in their children. Whilst schools can never act as an entirely effective substitute for the family, they can cultivate the positive attributes that many parents want to see developed in their children. The principal way in which these attributes are taught is through the example of a school's staff. Teachers must never discriminate against the children they teach or treat them unfairly. Schools should also be welcoming places for parents and members of the local community who should be seen as positive partners. Any partnership between parents and teachers should be based on mutual respect for the discrete qualities that each bring to their role – the partnership should be one of equal importance whilst the child is in school. Teachers need to work hard to establish good relations with parents and be aware that parents are particularly sensitive to negative comments made about their children. It is important to be constructive with parents in terms of all the forms of communication used to inform them about their child's progress. The partnership between home and school is a key factor in the success of each child's educational career.

6 Professional Relationships with Colleagues

Working successfully with colleagues is essential in any occupation. Good professional relationships have both organisational and personal dimensions. Productive working relationships are important for carrying out whatever organisational tasks need collaboration with others, but effective interactions at work are also very important contexts in which individual members of organisations satisfy basic personal, social and emotional needs.

Successful professional relationships have always been at the heart of the work of schools and teachers. It is no surprise that schools have increasingly sought to achieve the Investors in People Standard as a declaration of commitment to good practice in this area and as they seek to develop themselves as professional communities. Recent policy developments have placed new emphasis on teachers working with others in schools. The GTCE's Code of professional practice includes expectations which give teachers' work with others a certain kind of professional status. The government's policies for 'remodelling the workforce' (DfES, 2002a,b) are involving teachers in adjusting to two significant developments regarding those with whom they have routine interactions in school. The first is a planned increase in the numbers of Teaching Assistants (TAs) and the introduction of a new category of 'Higher Level Teaching Assistants', which will mean that more teachers than before will be working with more support in more classrooms. The second is represented by changes to teachers' conditions of service which are intended to pass to other people in schools a range of tasks and responsibilities which teachers have hitherto carried out themselves (DfES, 2003). Together, these developments significantly redraw the *formal* map of professional relationships in schools. More generally, policy trends over the last few years have increased the emphasis schools have to place on various forms of partnership and collaboration (Hargreaves, 1994; Helsby, 1999; Furlong *et al.*, 2000). Examples of this are: more active involvement of school governors in the day-to-day work of schools; appointing Co-ordinators for Key Stages and national strategy implementation, and the teamwork involved in these arrangements; formal partnerships with initial teacher training providers; and, in many cases, especially where schools have Beacon or other kinds of specialist status, relationships with neighbouring schools and other agencies and organisations in the wider community. Finally, and very much spurred by centrally driven school improvement and pupil achievement imperatives, schools are seeking to develop strong institutional identities and cultures informed by clear and agreed values – something which depends on sustained and effective staff collaborations. It also depends, quite critically, on a school's relationships with the parents and carers of its pupils.

So far as new teachers are concerned, Standard 1.6 refers to understanding 'the contribution that support staff and other professionals make to teaching and learning', and we will be looking at this particular issue in this chapter. But *several* of the Standards for QTS imply teachers' ability to work successfully in professional relationships with colleagues and partners. All of the Professional Values and Practice Standards are statutorily linked to the GTCE's professional Code, in which teachers are formally expected to 'respect the skills, expertise and contributions of these colleagues and partners', and to 'build productive working relationships with them in the interests of pupils'. The focus in the QTS Standards is almost entirely on how working with others contributes to pupils' learning. It is, however, essential to approach the business of developing good professional relationships against the much bigger policy and change agenda which we have just noted. For this reason, this chapter is not only about what the Standards expect. It offers perspectives on interacting with others in professional life which go beyond simply meeting the Standards.

The first section of the chapter addresses the importance, especially for new teachers, of focusing on professional relationships. The next section presents an overview of the range of professional relationships in which teachers are involved, and identifies in some detail the central features of working with TAs (with QTS Standard 1.6 in mind). The final section widens the angle of view to look at some of the personal resources needed in professional relationships and some key concepts and theoretical perspectives on interactions in the workplace. The twin aims of the chapter are to provide a conceptual framework in which to locate your experience of professional relationships, and to offer some practical guidance to help you make those relationships effective, satisfying and productive.

PROFESSIONAL RELATIONSHIPS IN TEACHER EDUCATION AND TRAINING

Initial teacher education and training tends to give priority to four 'families' of knowledge:

1   subject knowledge: the 'what' of teaching, the curriculum;
2   pedagogical knowledge: the 'why' and 'when' of teaching, the nature of learning;
3   technical knowledge: the 'how' of teaching, classroom methods and management; and
4   contextual knowledge: national policy frameworks, the organisation of schools, the teaching profession.

There is, however, a fifth 'family' of knowledge which includes moral and ethical dimensions of professional life, and the personal and interpersonal skills, aptitudes, capabilities and dispositions which make essential contributions to developing full professionalism as a teacher. It is worth noting that these personal attributes are the kind that headteachers often specifically ask about when requesting references on newly qualified teachers seeking appointments. We might call this fifth family of knowledge, 'personal and professional' knowledge.

It is a part of professionalism that does not always receive the same *systematic* and *explicit* attention in initial teacher training programmes as the other kinds of professional knowledge, and has hitherto been somewhat neglected in the literature intended specifically for new teachers on training courses. This is especially the case where the topic of professional relationships is concerned. Where the subject has been addressed in the professional literature, it is typically in texts on school organisation and leadership aimed at those in management positions and students of educational policy and administration, but even these say little about the interpersonal skills involved in effective professional relationships. Some research studies explore staff relationships in schools in ways which new teachers will find illuminating, like those of Nias *et al.* (1989), or the chapter devoted to 'Teachers' Working Relationships' in one of the volumes in the PACE (Primary Assessment, Curriculum and Experience) series of studies (Osborn *et al.*, 2000). But there is very little literature indeed which treats what we are calling personal and professional knowledge in much detail. It sometimes seems that teachers embarking on professional life are assumed to possess or be able to develop intuitively abilities like 'the capacity to relate with colleagues and to work collaboratively with them' (Dillon and Maguire, 2001). On the other hand, there are many books on improving personal effectiveness aimed at a general readership, and there is scholarly literature in the field of business management which often includes much that is potentially helpful to teachers about workplace interactions. We will be drawing on both kinds of literature later.

If there is a gap in the professional literature it is all the more surprising when you consider how central – and sometimes challenging – this area of professional life can be for new teachers. Occasionally it becomes a really critical factor in school-based experience or in completing a course of training. Virtually everything we do as teachers is deeply and unavoidably influenced by underlying personal capabilities, so it is surprising that these capabilities are not always addressed directly and systematically, except, perhaps, when they emerge as difficulties for particular individuals. We should remember that until 2002, this area of professional competence did not feature prominently in the statutory requirements for teachers' professional education and training. It may also be felt that it is psychological and emotional territory which should remain 'private', or that it is not possible to 'train' people in such personal and subjective areas. If so, it is a misplaced view, and one which is not supported by the evidence of what people completing courses of initial teacher training say about the quite profound impact the experience has on them *as people*. Here are a couple of representative voices:

> 'The development of self-awareness, the need to reflect continually on your own working practices in order to improve, change and adapt...'

> 'I would strongly recommend the course to anyone interested in learning about themselves, their capabilities, strengths and weaknesses, and in how to unlock their potential...'
>
> Post Graduate Certificate in Education (PGCE) Students

The references to change, adaptation and learning about oneself in these comments remind us that training to be a teacher is, fundamentally and very importantly, a process of 'socialisation' into a particular professional group or culture. The concept of socialisation has expanded from its early applications in studies of children growing up in societies, to be applied to new members (sometimes called 'novices') entering occupations and professions such as teaching. One formal academic definition of socialisation is:

> the process whereby individuals become members of society or members of sectors of society. It is concerned with how individuals adopt, or do not adopt, the values, customs and perspectives of the surrounding culture or subculture.
>
> (Husen and Postlethwiate, 1994: 5586)

One dictionary, reflecting what is now an outdated view of socialisation as a process 'done to' largely passive subjects, defines it as 'the process by which people, especially children, are made to behave in ways that are acceptable in their culture or society'. Trainee teachers may sometimes feel that they are too much being 'made to behave' in certain ways, but we hope that this is only transitory! A much more subtle and complex view of 'socialisation-as-interaction' is presented by William Wentworth (Wentworth, 1980). In this perspective, the novice is *actively involved* in shaping and influencing the very society they are entering. As Wentworth puts it, the novice 'helps to forge the socialising experience'. To bring this right into the realm of the teaching profession, each trainee teacher assimilates certain attributes he or she identifies as being characteristic of 'teachers' from school experience or from other parts of the training experience (and, we should remember, from their own considerable knowledge of schools and teaching as former pupils themselves, which makes socialisation into *teaching* a rather special case compared with other professions). However, by their very presence in these settings; by what they do and think; and as novice members of the culture they are joining, they actually put their own mark on what characterises that culture and its values and practices. The interaction is bi-directional and mutual. The culture influences the novice; the novice influences the culture; each interaction continually shifts and alters the very conditions in which the process of socialisation occurs.

This helps to explain two quite different features of initial teacher education: why schools generally welcome novice teachers on school-based experience (because they frequently 'refresh' the professional culture in the host school); and why it is often difficult to provide decisive advice about certain kinds of situations which confront trainee teachers. Good mentoring often needs to be highly tentative and a process of exploring possible alternative courses of action rather than proposing a single 'right and true way'. Each situation is uniquely the outcome of a particular combination of circumstances or events, and its resolution is likely to be dependent on several variable factors. This can be very frustrating for the trainee who wants a decisive and 'ready-made' solution, but it is absolutely consistent with the insights which this concept of socialisation-as-interaction gives us into the complex nature of professional learning.

TASK

Professional dilemmas

To make this a little clearer, consider these two real examples of professional relationship problems encountered by two different student teachers. You might like to cover up the questions which follow them first, so that you can think about each problem for a few moments free from any kind of prompting of your thoughts.

Problem 1

I was assisting the class teacher. The class teacher shared the class with an NQT. A couple of the class began to criticise the NQT's teaching. The class teacher responded by explicitly criticising the NQT (not present) further and, less bluntly, agreeing with the class. I felt very uncomfortable listening to this as I would deem it unprofessional behaviour. Problems with the NQT's teaching style were a common topic of conversation amongst the rest of the department, but discussion there was confined to the staff.

Problem 2

I share a class which is in the normal class teacher's room. She has arranged the classroom so that it is impossible to move between some tables to get to the pupils. I find this layout impossible to teach in effectively. She says she has arranged the tables so that pupils do not write on walls and does not want me to move them. She is also my mentor and will be observing my lessons. How can I resolve this?

Here are the questions. Take some time out to think about these questions before you read on.

Problem 1

If you were the trainee teacher, what, if anything would you do in this situation:

(a)   regarding your professional relationship with the class teacher/mentor?
(b)   regarding your professional relationship with the NQT?
(c)   regarding your professional relationships with other members of the department?

Problem 2

How would you advise this student if you were their teacher training course tutor?

There are, we suggest, no simple and straightforward solutions. The problems themselves are challengingly intractable. The first raises some quite serious ethical issues about the propriety of discussing others' practice either in front of pupils, whether or not the other is present, or in private – if indeed the department office or a staffroom is professionally 'private'. There is, too, the question of how and whether the trainee teacher can, might or should react. The minimal response would be, of course, to do nothing. But no doubt the trainee may very well be wondering whether, if that class teacher talks about the NQT's practice with pupils, they might also be discussing his or her own teaching with them. The second problem about preferred classroom layouts is at first sight more purely 'technical', but it is just as difficult an issue, especially in terms of relationships. The trainee is being baulked from trying to teach in the way he or she sees appropriate, and feels trapped by a particular kind of professional relationship with the teacher, with all the tricky issues of power and status that this relationship includes. Should the trainee personally insist on a different layout? If so, are there risks in terms of the mentor's appraisal of the trainee? Would it be better to seek the course tutor's intervention? Should the trainee just get on with it without making a fuss?

Trainee teachers face situations like this where professional relationships are loaded with all kinds of rather special sensitivities and contingencies simply because of the conditions attaching to their position in schools: as novices, under intensive assessment, and very temporary. Special though they are as situations, they illustrate all too dramatically the interpersonal skills and inner resources that are required in managing all relationships, and hence the importance of putting this dimension of professional knowledge firmly on to the training agenda. It is an area in which individuals can consciously learn and develop their own skills and abilities, and where support and guidance are available, based on well-founded knowledge about interactions in occupational settings.

Professional relationships in schools: an overview

What kinds of professional relationships are typical in a teacher's normal work? Apart from support staff, who are the 'other professionals' to which Standard 1.6 refers? What follows is an overview of a wide range of categories of people with whom teachers work. It is deliberately inclusive of some who may not be involved in contributing directly to teaching and learning in the sense intended by Standard 1.6. The list introduces a basic form of differentiation between many kinds of 'other professionals' by grouping them according to whether they are members of the school staff, occasional visitors to the school, or located off-site and mainly visited by teachers (with pupils). Those who are members of the school staff are further subdivided into two groups reflecting the regularity or frequency with which teachers can expect to interact with them. Both factors (location and frequency of contact) are important determinants of the kind of professional relationships which can be established and have implications for the range of personal skills needed.

School staff: regular contact	*In a secondary school* Subject department colleagues Head of Department or Faculty Key Stage Co-ordinator(s) Teachers in other subject departments Modern Foreign Languages (MFL): Language Assistants *In a primary school* Teachers in your own Key Stage/Year team Teachers in other Key Stage/Year teams Subject Leaders/Key Stage Co-ordinators

	Headteacher/Deputy headteacher
	All schools
	ITT Mentor, NQT Induction Tutor, Staff Development Co-ordinator
	Special Education Needs Co-ordinator (SENCO)
	Head of Year or division. Class/form Tutors in same division
	Information and Communications Technology (ICT) Co-ordinator
	Teaching Assistants
	Administrative Support Staff and Clerical Assistants
	Librarian/Learning Resources staff
	Resources and other Technicians
School staff: occasional contact	Caretaker/Premises/Business managers
	Midday Supervisors
	School Nurse
	In most secondary schools
	Headteacher and Deputy headteachers
Visitors to school	Supply Teachers
	Visiting specialists providing curriculum input, e.g. authors, musicians, artists, sportspersons, Theatre in Education groups, Police, Community Volunteers/ Officers, Business and Industry people
	Ethnic Minority Achievement Services (EMAS) and English as an Additional Language (EAL) support staff
	Parents/Guardians
	Careers Advisers
	Student Mentors and Teacher Associates, young adults on work experience or pre-teacher training experience
	Connexions/Youth Service personnel
	Educational Psychologists
	Educational Welfare Officers
	LEA Advisers/Inspectors
	School Governors
	OFSTED Inspectors
	Education researchers
Off-site personnel	Field Study Centre personnel
	Museum/Heritage Centre Education personnel
	Library Service personnel
	Science, Technology and Arts Centre Education Officers

Note: The list could be extended, but these are probably the main categories of people with whom all teachers have contact.

What is immediately obvious is the very wide variety of people and roles involved, and hence the diversity of relationships in which teachers engage.

In order to get things into perspective it is helpful to consider three generic 'dimensions' of this diversity which all professional relationships share:

1 the relationship's purpose;
2 the relative positions or status of those involved in a given relationship; and
3 the personal histories and interpersonal skills the parties involved bring to the relationship.

Dimension 1: Purpose and function of the relationship

One dimension of diversity in relationships is the variety of purposes and reasons for having contact with different kinds of people and, to put it more directly, the nature of the 'agendas' which bring people together in the first place. The purposes of contact with parents of the children you teach are very different from the purposes informing contact with, say, a Teaching Assistant you work with regularly. Questions to bear in mind, then, include:

• Why is this relationship part of my work as a teacher?
• What are the really central items on my agenda?
• What is likely to be the other party's agenda, and what can I do to be more knowledgeable about this?
• What do I want as the outcome(s) from this relationship?
• What particular skills, attitudes or perspectives do I have, or might I need to develop, to support the functions of this relationship?

Dimension 2: Status and position in the relationship

Another dimension relates to status, position and accountability. Contact with an OFSTED Inspector, for example, is on a very different basis in this respect from contact with a teaching colleague. Degrees of status vary quite significantly even between teaching colleagues, depending on experience, formal position, role designations and even the basic matter of age. Sometimes such factors introduce complex dynamics into relationships, such as when a mature trainee teacher with many years of experience outside education, and accustomed to line management responsibilities for more junior colleagues, has to adjust to being intensively managed, supervised and assessed themselves during school-based initial training or induction as an NQT, quite possibly by someone many years younger. Issues of power-relations inevitably intrude. How this impinges on trainee teachers can swing from one extreme to another quite dramatically. At one moment you may be in sole charge of a class of thirty children, vested with all the responsibility and authority for managing a teaching relationship with them and for managing the contributions of one or more TAs for an hour or so. The next you may be thrust into the position of learner yourself for feedback from an observer, requiring a completely different set of dispositions and responses in a mentoring relationship. The shifts involved in handling both situations are demanding. Questions include:

- What is my status and position in this relationship?
- What is the other party's status and position?
- If there is a significant difference between my position and the other party's, what implications arise for how I conduct myself?
- Do I need to 'rehearse' (or even 'research' and practise) any strategies or techniques which will help to reduce any difficulties that that difference presents?
- What might I set out to learn from this relationship that advances my abilities to handle professional relationships?

Dimension 3: Personal histories and interpersonal skills brought into relationships

Another important dimension is represented by the very varied personal histories and skills that every individual brings into any relationship. The more formal (and more infrequent) contact is with someone, the more likely it is that these histories are not known, shared and mutually understood, and scope for misreading the 'other' can develop. Our personal histories profoundly inform professional relationships, though there are some aspects of personal life which should be kept entirely separate. A *necessary* combination of personal and professional interests in professional relationships was emphasised at the very beginning of this chapter, but maintaining a balance between the 'private' (or personal) self and the 'public' (or professional) self is at the heart of what is often popularly meant by 'behaving in a professional way'. Success in keeping *an appropriate balance* between the two – a balance which will not always be the same in every relationship – depends on accurately assessing where 'private' and 'public' worlds begin and end, and on the way you see the other 'dimensions' of a particular relationship. This is not at all an easy judgement to make, and misjudgements about where the boundaries between personal and professional lie are frequently the sources of strain (or worse) in professional relationships. Questions include:

- What interpersonal skills and previous experience help me in this relationship?
- What traits or tendencies do I have which I may need to be consciously alert to and curb?
- What are my strategies and opportunities for understanding where the other party 'is coming from', and how will I use this knowledge if I get it?
- What boundaries will I set in this relationship to sustain a completely professional approach?
- What will I do if, for whatever reason, those boundaries are threatened?

The questions attached to each of these three dimensions are plain enough in themselves. Answering them, though, and taking appropriate action on the basis of the answers, calls for an extensive repertoire of personal resources, understanding and some theoretical knowledge to support effective professional relationships. The final part of this chapter picks this up, but the immediate next step is to identify the salient features of what is involved in the professional relationship when teachers work with TAs.

We concentrate exclusively on TAs partly because this is the main focus of QTS Standard 1.6, and partly as an example to represent professional relationships generally. It will become clear that this is not advice about *how to manage* a professional relationship. It is what needs to come *before* that: analysing the functions that a relationship serves, and conceptualising the sorts of capabilities or practices that the functions involve. It is by no means an exhaustive list, but it covers the most essential aspects of a teacher's work with a TA.

Teachers working with Teaching Assistants: professional relationship functions

- making/finding time for collaborative planning and post-teaching review; personal organisation, time management and scheduling;
- reaching agreement about the purposes and nature of the support, and how the TA's support complements and extends the teacher's;
- facilitating liaison between the TA (and the teacher) and the SENCO, particularly where a TA has Individual Education Plan (IEP)-related roles with individual pupils. 'Because they often spend more time with some pupils than the teacher does, assistants working with children with special educational needs may well have important contributions to make to their individual educational plans' (DfES, 2000);

- sharing feedback on teaching and learning (teacher to TA, TA to teacher, pupils to both). This depends on establishing a climate of mutual confidence and trust with TAs;
- understanding each other's particular skills and strengths, and exploiting them effectively. This really only comes from 'getting to know' each other, and being mutually open about personal strengths and limitations;
- encouraging the TA to function 'with confidence and . . . exercise their own judgement' (DfES, 2000). This calls for being able to demonstrate that you value the TA's work, and can be helped by planning with them occasions when they take a 'lead' role;
- enabling the TA to feel, and be seen by pupils to be, a full member of the teaching team in lessons, and not marginalised. This is easier when, particularly in primary schools, the TA is always or regularly present. When this is not the case, as in many secondary lessons, you may need to create ways of deliberately 'including' TAs by, for example, inviting them to offer contributions in, say, a questioning routine;
- managing the balance between leading and delegating. This clearly lies at the heart of a good teacher/TA relationship. Many of the other factors included in this section are, essentially, key determinants in achieving a successful balance;
- agreeing behaviour management policies/routines, and respective roles and responsibilities, 'so that conflicting messages are not given to pupils. This includes the TA knowing the limits of tolerance the teacher will apply to individual pupils' (DfES, 2000). Importantly, it involves not expecting a TA to exercise authority which you do not have yourself, or are not prepared to exercise;
- respecting TAs' contractual conditions of service (hours employed, pay, commitments elsewhere in school, etc.), and understanding a TA's personal circumstances, priorities and interests. Sensitivity to this is important. TAs' conditions of service vary from school to school, and even from one to another in the same school. Most are paid by the hour of actual classroom work, and some are funded for very specific purposes (such as to support a given pupil under special needs arrangements). This immediately places limits on the scope for 'out-of-hours' planning and review. It is also important to recognise that many TAs very deliberately choose the assistant rather than a full teaching role (Lee and Mawson, 1998). The basis of every good workplace relationship is knowledge of the structure and framework within which it exists, and *not* making what could be false assumptions out of ignorance of these factors;
- ensuring parents fully understand TA roles and activities. This is more a matter for policy adopted by the whole school, but as an individual teacher you can do a lot to support it. Including the observations of

a TA on individual pupils they have worked closely with in reports and discussions with parents is one example; another is keeping parents informed about work you are doing with classes, including contributions made to it by TAs. Parents of children identified as qualifying for special support will almost certainly know about it, but where TAs have more general class-wide roles it is wise to ensure that all parents are aware of the arrangements;

- ensuring that 'the way in which the TA works does not form a barrier to a pupil's participation in experiences and learning with peers' (Balshaw and Farrell, 2002). Highly valuable as individualised support can be, pupils need to experience inclusion in the whole class or group and develop the social skills involved in collaborating with their peers. The fact that an individual pupil may have a TA alongside them should not mean that they are never 'brought into' whole-class work. Indeed, it can provide the context for the TA's most valuable and focused work with individual pupils. Be on guard, then, against any tendency to leave out 'supported' pupils from whole-class and sub-group activities;

- supporting TAs' inclusion in wider professional (and staff social) activity (e.g. Key Stage/Year/Department meetings, school In-service education and training (INSET), working groups), so far as contractual conditions permit. This is also more a matter of school policy, but teachers can be proactive in planning joint inputs to meetings with TAs. As research has shown (Farrell *et al.*, 2000), TAs welcome this kind of professional inclusion, and schools are increasingly extending TAs' contractual arrangements to cover it; and

- periodic reviews of the teacher/TA classroom relationship; 'This…could include practical issues such as how the classroom is organised physically so as to help them best fulfil their roles' (DfES, 2000).

It would be a useful exercise to do the same kind of analysis for selected other categories of people in the overview presented earlier. It could be the basis of an activity for trainee teachers working under the guidance of the Senior Professional Tutor in school. Whether or not it is formally organised in that way, it is worth thinking about doing something like this as a way of putting together for a QTS professional portfolio evidence of achievement of QTS Standard 1.6. The Standard, remember, requires an *understanding* of the contribution that 'support staff and other professionals make to teaching and learning'. The *Qualifying to Teach: Handbook of Guidance* (TTA, 2003), makes quite clear that the Standard 'does not…require trainee teachers to demonstrate an ability to undertake a supervisory role independently', but that 'they should be developing the skills they will need to collaborate with and manage other team members as the situation demands…'. The first skill involved in this is being clear about the functions of the collaboration and what actually needs to be 'managed'. This kind of analysis will develop that skill.

Professional relationships: personal resources, concepts and theoretical perspectives

It was suggested earlier in the chapter that the literature on business management is a source of information and guidance about relationships in the workplace. More precisely, it is the literature on interactions in the workplace which is most helpful. This section offers some key perspectives, drawing on what is probably the most authoritative and comprehensive survey of current research and scholarship in this area (Guirdham, 2002). Guirdham's work, under the title *Interpersonal skills at work* in its first two editions, but now called *Interactive behaviour at work*, is primarily a textbook for students on Business and Management programmes such as the MBA. Its examples, scenarios and exercises almost entirely relate to commercially orientated organisations, but its outline of fundamental concepts and its coverage of topics such as conflict resolution and communication skills are applicable to all occupational settings, including schools. This section also draws on a very different kind of book: Kris Cole's *The complete idiot's guide to clear communication* (Cole, K., 2002). Cole's book is recommended – and not just for helping with professional relationships. You should not be at all put off by its 'trendy' title as part of a well-known and widely sold series. You will get a lot from it that you can use in the classroom (and in life generally). We will be sliding from one source to the other in what follows, merging theoretical perspectives, conceptual understandings and practical 'no frills' advice from both of them.

Early in her book Guirdham (2002: 82) points to the fundamental importance of understanding the psychological factors which underpin people's behaviour:

> we need to try to understand values, motives, goals, emotions, beliefs, attitudes, intentions, abilities and traits if we are to understand and predict our own and other people's behaviour and to improve our own interpersonal skills.

This sets appropriately widely the arena in which any guidance on professional relationships must be located. Emotional intelligence, for example, has recently become recognised as a critical ability, and Guirdham cites the definition of this concept by its originators as 'an ability to recognize the meanings of emotions and to reason and problem solve on the basis of them'. Being able to 'tune in' to other people's feelings, and to manage our own, are essential interpersonal skills.

Guirdham is emphatic that 'being good at dealing with people is not just a capacity that someone either has or lacks, an unalterable facet of personality'. 'Learning',

Guirdham (2002: 140) writes, 'is the key to how interpersonal skills develop.' This echoes what was said earlier in this chapter about interactions in occupational settings being an area of professional knowledge which can be consciously learned, and, interestingly, Guirdham too makes the connection with socialisation:

> For most people, starting college or work, even a change of job, requires new learning about how to behave – new socialisation.

In one of many summaries of advice distilling other published studies, she suggests the following as the approaches and attitudes that can be studied, understood and practised to aid this learning:

- 'Aim to have a broad repertoire of ways of dealing with people'. Guirdham points to the danger of 'becoming increasingly imprisoned in one or two ways of behaving and therefore of being unable to deal effectively with situations which really need a different approach.' Versatility and flexibility are thus central.
- 'Know about the factors that affect interpersonal behaviour and be aware of what goes on when people interact. This is called *mindfulness*…'. Mindfulness is defined as 'not being locked into habitual ways of categorising others, being open to new information…and being aware of more than one perspective'. Valuable advice.
- 'Know yourself better – be more aware of your own strengths, weaknesses, prejudices and the impression you give.'
- 'Be more aware of others – more sensitive to their emotions and attitudes and a better judge of their motives and abilities. Carefully observing others helps this learning once you know what to look for.'
- 'Practise your skills, ideally where there is little risk and where feedback is available.'

Unfortunately, of course, the circumstances of teacher training are such that the sites for practising are quite heavily laden with 'risk', since no part of the normal business of schools is, as it were, suspended to permit inconsequential rehearsal of skills. It used to be called 'teaching *practice*'; now it is 'school-based experience', with levels of accountability very little different from those applied to fully qualified professionals. Trainee teachers, as we have seen in a couple of examples, find themselves in professional relationships that are as real – and as full of consequence – as any established teacher. Because of this it is essential to approach the matter of developing positive professional relationships just as purposefully as any other aspect of training: by actively seeking guidance from tutors and mentors; by talking to and witnessing the practice of other people; by reading; and by reflecting on and documenting personal experience.

Guirdham suggests that there are five 'core skills'. They are adopted here as an overall framework for considering what goes into professional relationships:

- understanding others;
- self-presentation;
- communicating;
- persuading; and
- using power.

Understanding others

Understanding others includes: attending to others and interpreting verbal and non-verbal cues they provide; making attributions ('deciding the 'cause' of what someone is doing'), and forming judgements and impressions; being aware of cultural, ethnic and gender influences; thinking about how the other person may be 'framing', or making their own sense of a particular situation. Much of this involves 'de-centering' yourself, or putting yourself in the other person's position. Fundamentally, it involves listening.

Active listening and what Cole calls 'Reflective Listening' (Cole, K., 2002: 158) are key component skills in understanding others. Cole offers these tips for listening:

- Develop patience. Practise paying attention to the person speaking to you;
- Push away any internal dialogue and stay focused on listening;
- Listen to understand what the person is really saying;
- Listen to, not against;
- Observe body language. Listen for what is not said;
- Take your lesson from the Chinese *ting*: listen with your eyes, mind and heart, as well as your ears;
- 'Send back' what you have heard to verify it by restating the speaker's meaning and/or their feelings in your own words;
- Match the speaker's tempo and tone in your own responses; and
- Remember, you do not need to agree, just understand things from the speaker's perspective.

Self-presentation

Self-presentation (or 'impression management') is all about 'how we produce intended or unintended effects on the minds of those with whom we interact at work' (Guirdham, 2002). These are among Guirdham's proposals, citing other work, for creating a 'generally favourable impression':

- Use a degree of openness. Make a disclosure, but avoid intimate revelations too soon in a relationship;
- Show liking for the other person. This is undoubtedly the most powerful way of being liked in return;
- Show similarity with the other person;
- Try 'stroking'. This can be done through body language – visibly listening, nodding, not interrupting and keeping your gaze under control;
- Adopt some aspect of the communication style of the other person;
- Resist the temptation to put the other person right on small, irrelevant facts; and
- Allow for cultural differences.

The final point is not, as it may seem, politically incorrect. In the matters of gesture and facial expression (especially), body languages are culturally different just like verbal languages. Misunderstandings can also stem from false assumptions being made about the meaning or significance of key ideas or words.

While these points about self-presentation may suggest some practical strategies for creating a 'favourable impression', they do not really touch on the central issue, which is how they add up to conveying to others in professional relationships our core values, beliefs and attitudes. Much more is involved in self-presentation than strategies and techniques. Professional relationships test our opinions and values, our prejudices and preferences, our knowledge and experience, our motivations and inclinations, even though all of these may be very uncertain and in high states of flux during the professional socialisation process. Nevertheless, despite the uncertainty, presenting the 'self' calls for elements of clarity and decisiveness to give direction and purpose to the ways we work with others. The trick is to be clear and decisive, without appearing arrogant, opinionated, or, above all, closed against the possibility – indeed, *probability* – of adjusting our ideas as experience or knowledge increases. Professional relationships – interactions with people generally – are never as productive and successful as they could be when one of those involved presents themselves as fixed and intransigent. Decisiveness is one thing. Bigotry is quite another.

Communicating

Communicating, quite clearly, is the vehicle which carries all relationships, or, rather, the fleet of vehicles, because we communicate in a variety of ways, each of which challenges us differently: listening, speaking, writing (on paper and electronically), non-verbally, by our actions, appearance and behaviour. It is a huge subject and one we can only touch on here. Cole's book, or anything similar on personal communication skills, offers much more help.

Some remarks about listening have already been made, so we will jump straight to speaking. The first thing to say is something obvious but nevertheless important: talk is central. As Nias *et al.* (1989) succinctly put it, 'Chat is a high-level activity':

> Two related features of the collaborative schools were that the staff spent a great deal of time talking to one another and that their conversations were usually a mixture of chat about themselves and discussion of their teaching.

Guirdham (2002: 420) also notes the interdependence of social/personal and occupational/professional interaction:

> In work relationships ... those concerned interact partly as individual personalities but also as occupants of positions and performers of roles.

It is good to have that kind of endorsement of the value of social chat, reminding us that good professional relationships are dependent on much more than exclusive concentration on 'professional' matters. Workplace relationships which are devoid of any social dimension are sterile.

Without going into very fine detail, what tips are there for developing good speaking habits? It is probably wrong to answer such a question with what 'not to do', but Cole, K. (2002: 166) offers these 'Ten Deadly Sins of Communication' to avoid:

Patronising sins:
1   Evaluating,
2   Moralising,
3   Playing psychologist or labelling, and
4   Making sarcastic remarks.

Sending signals sins:
5   Commanding,
6   Railroading,
7   Threatening, and
8   Giving unsolicited advice.

Avoiding sins:
9   Being vague, and
10   Diverting.

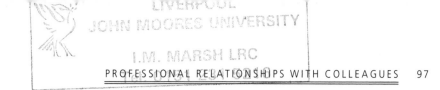
More positively, here is a selection from Cole's many suggested skills, strategies and techniques for clear verbal communication:

Frame your conversations	a framing statement indicates what will be addressed and what will not be, drawing attention to the main aspects. Examples are: • boundaries: what will and will not be focused on; • history: reviewing the key events that have a bearing on the conversation; • purposes: presenting expectations and checking whether the other person shares them; • process: outlining a suggested way of proceeding; and • problem: stating the nature of a problem, and the evidence bearing on it.
Flagging	'prompts' which help the other person to see the direction in which you are going, and *vice versa*. Examples: • 'If I've understood you correctly...'; • 'Let me ask you...'; and • 'So, to sum it all up...'.
Choose positive words and phrases	Negative words and phrases, compared with positive ones, draw quite different responses from people. Examples (negative first): • 'You'll have to...' v. 'You'll want to...'; • 'I can't do that until Monday...' v. 'I'll be able to do that on Monday...'; • 'What's the problem?...' v. 'How can I help?...' • 'I can't because...' v. 'Here's how we can make that happen...'
Choose words that reflect the six C's	• clear; • concise; • complete; • courteous; • correct; and • concrete.
Speak clearly	No comment.
Use people's names	...but not over-frequently, which can easily sound slick and patronising.
Provide examples	...or metaphors or analogies. This helps to make ideas more concrete and memorable.
Use the other person's 'language'	...to build rapport and respect.
Speak for yourself	Generally good advice, but (and it's an important 'but') in group situations where collaborating and reaching a consensus with others are prime purposes, constantly saying 'I think...' and 'I do...' can seriously grate on others, and be counter-collaborative.
Don't sidetrack yourself	...into irrelevant asides diverting from the main point.

| Ask rather than tell | Telling is pushy. Prefer, for example, 'I really need to have that ready by tomorrow morning. Would that be possible for you?' rather than 'I want that ready by tomorrow morning.' |
| Persuade, do not pressure | Persuasion is always a gentler option. Master three skills to be persuasive:
• earning credibility;
• gathering good information; and
• giving good information. |

Face-to-face communication is critically influenced by body language, sometimes termed 'non-verbal communication'. Actually, as Mehrabian points out, both terms are a bit exclusive, particularly of the vitally important element of vocal tone or expression, which is neither 'body' language nor, in a sense, 'non-verbal'. He prefers the more inclusive term 'implicit communication', and his really fascinating book extends to discussions of, for example, the influences the physical environment and the arrangement of furniture can have on interactions between people (Mehrabian, 1981).

Cole, K. (2002: 104–110) devotes the whole of Part 3 of his book to body language and voice, and says, 'the way we deliver a message accounts for up to 93% of its meaning'. 'Implicit communication' is also important in how we receive messages; we 'read' the signals given out by those with whom we talk. He offers a mnemonic 'to help you remember the seven main aspects of managing your body language':

SO CLEAR

S   is for the way you *sit* or *stand* and the way you use *space*.
O   is for the *openness* of your expression or movements.
C   is for how you *center your attention* on the other person.
L   is for how you *lean* to show attention, apply pressure or reduce pressure.
E   is for the way you make *eye contact*.
A   is for how *at ease* you are when you communicate.
R   is for how well we *reflect* and *respond* to what the speaker has said.

Whatever the exact magnitude of the contribution made by body language or 'implicit communication' to communicating with others, there is no doubt that it is very significant – and very powerful. It merits serious study and, of course, there are countless opportunities to do so. If you want to take it further, there are many readily available books aimed at a general readership on body language, and at least one (Neill, 1993) expressly intended for teachers.

Persuading

The Sections 'Persuading' and 'Using power' both are about influencing in Guirdham's conceptualisation of core skills for interaction. As she points out, 'Most accounts of influencing do not distinguish between *persuading* and *power*', but her distinction is helpful, particularly since – outside the classroom at least – trainee teachers rarely find themselves in positions of power in professional relationships, except possibly as the targets of that power. Guirdham (2002: 320) characterises the difference as follows:

> Persuading [means] exerting influence over others by means other
> than using power, including discussion, argument, conveying liking and
> other communication actions…Power means influencing others through
> using the ability to control their outcomes, in other words, to affect
> what happens to them, for example through rewards and punishments.

Among the suggestions Guirdham (2002: 336) makes on 'How to increase your effectiveness at changing others' attitudes' are:

- Apply moderate rather than extreme pressure;
- Pay attention to the target person's attitude to *yourself*, not just the topic you are concerned with. Emphasise similarity;
- Stress the benefits of new ideas and introduce them incrementally;
- Avoid trying to change attitudes that are central, consistent and intense;
- Work to increase your credibility as a persuasive source;
- Rehearse. If possible, try role-playing with a friend; and
- Be persistent.

Persuading is very often the handmaiden of resolving conflict and negotiation, both of which are needed from time to time in professional relationships. A classic study of the latter, written at a popular level and well worth looking at, is Roger Fisher and William Ury's *Getting to yes*, whose sub-title is, '*Negotiating an agreement without giving in*' (Fisher and Ury, 1999). Conflict resolution (or conflict management) is a major field of study in its own right. One interesting model (cited by both Guirdham, 2002, and Cole, K., 2002) identifies five styles of handling conflict, each of which reflects different relative levels of concern with one's own needs or the needs of others (as shown in the figure):

Source: Guirdham, 2002, p. 431, adapted from Thomas, K.W. (1976) *Conflict and conflict management*, in M.D. Dunette (ed.), *Handbook of Industrial and Organization Psychology*, Chicago, Ill., Rand McNally. With permission of Houghton Miflin Co.

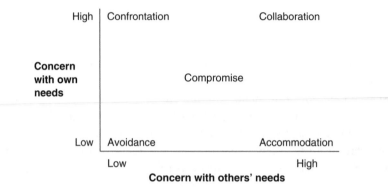

- *Confrontation* – high on concern with one's own needs but low on concern with others' needs: involving, for example, demanding apologies from others and redress of perceived wrongs;
- *Accommodation* – high on concern with others' needs but low on concern with one's own needs: apologising and conceding the issue to the other person regardless of the 'rights and wrongs' of the matter;
- *Avoidance* – low on concern with both own and others' needs: refusing to acknowledge a problem exists, while reducing interaction with the other person(s) as far as possible;
- *Collaboration* – high on concern with both own and others' needs: involving an approach that treats the conflict as a problem that the parties need to solve together; and
- *Compromise* – equal in concern with both own and others' needs: bargaining, explicitly or implicitly, with the other person until a compromise is reached.

As Guirdham (2002: 431) points out,

> Confrontation, avoidance and accommodation are all, in their different ways, undesirable, tending to reinforce the conflict and create more ill-feeling, to prolong it below the surface or to encourage further aggression in others. Both compromising and collaborative styles are more effective than these, though in compromises there is the well-known danger that the actual compromise agreed on will be the worst of all worlds.

Before we leave conflict management, think back to the two professional dilemmas reported by PGCE students which we looked at earlier in this chapter and consider the following questions:

1   Which of the five conflict-handling styles was your preference in each scenario?
2   Does this model of different ways of handling conflict colour the kind of advice you would now give as the course tutor to the student with the classroom layout problem?
3   When faced with conflicts of this kind, which style(s) do you personally tend to adopt?
4   Which do you find hardest?
5   What aspects of your own conflict-handling skills do you think you need to work on?

Using power

As we saw in discussing general dimensions of all professional relationships, power and status (and authority) are issues. The position of trainee teachers is, to say the least, somewhat ambiguous so far as this is concerned. They hold little or no 'positional' power (that which 'goes with' particular roles and positions in an organisation) except with regard to pupils – and then to some extent only conditionally. They rely almost entirely on 'personal' power (that which they generate through their own professional conduct, social relations and expertise). This is not to suggest that they are permanently consigned to occupying positions of low power in all professional relationships they engage in. Guirdham's use of the term 'power' is very much conditioned by the business management context in which she writes, and it is, as she begins her discussion of the concept by pointing out, 'a complex notion [which] cannot simply be accounted for in a single definition'.

   The most efficacious kind of power that new teachers (especially trainee teachers on school experience), can command is the power that flows from demonstrating dedication and application to the business of 'learning the trade'. Others who are well established in their professional lives and work will expect new teachers to display those qualities, and that includes some degree of deference to greater experience, positive acceptance of the value of advice and guidance, and readiness to act on that guidance. If, in the course of displaying these characteristics, a novice teacher *also* demonstrates through their work certain levels of professional achievement and success as a classroom teacher and colleague, *then* that novice teacher has earned something in the currency of power which can be spent in transactions with professional colleagues. It would be an unwise, if not downright arrogant, novice teacher who did not take this fully on board into the professional relationships they engage in during initial training and early career experience.

There is a clue in what has just been said to a possible resolution of our PGCE student's classroom layout problem, and we end this chapter with one final question about it. That problem is, after all, essentially a problem arising from the unequal distribution of power between the student and the class teacher/mentor. Using the monetary metaphor of *currency* and *transaction* we have just deployed, and putting yourself in that student's situation, what coins in the currency of professional 'power' (metaphorically speaking) would you try to have in your 'professional bank' in order to complete the transaction with the mentor to your satisfaction of moving the tables?

Conclusion

We began this chapter by noting that *successful* professional relationships are needed both *strategically* (to maximise task or role effectiveness) and *personally* (to maximise personal job satisfaction). The circumstances in which teachers are increasingly working mean that the ability to engage in *productive* professional relationships is a central feature of professionalism which needs to be directly addressed in initial training and early career development. By looking at the wide range of people teachers routinely work with, and by analysing in some detail the example of teachers' work with TAs who are supporting them in the classroom, we have explored the *diversity* of what is involved in establishing professional relationships in schools. Finally, some of the essential features contributing to *practical personal effectiveness* in professional relationships have been indicated, locating these within a five-point *conceptual framework* for thinking about interaction with others at work.

TASK

Understanding a particular professional relationship

The purpose of this exercise is to apply some of the ideas in this chapter to a professional relationship in which you are involved. There are two aims in this: first, to practise thinking systematically about professional relationships as a general habit of professional life; and second, to develop a particular relationship you are involved in so that it is as successful and constructive as possible.

Look back to the three dimensions of professional relationships in the section headed 'Professional relationships in schools: an overview'. Choose one particular relationship which is significant in your professional work in school. Under three headings corresponding to the three dimensions (1: Purpose and function of the relationship; 2: Status and position in the relationship; 3: Personal histories and interpersonal skills brought into the relationship), work through each of the questions which are presented in the bullet points for each dimension.

Answer each question with very brief notes. Sometimes single words will be sufficient; but some of them may need two or three phrases or a sentence or two. Do this entirely privately: there is no need to share it with anyone.

When you have done this you should be more fully and explicitly aware of the 'dynamics' of that particular relationship, and how you can maximise its benefits – primarily for yourself, but probably also for the other person. The final step is to put into practice what the exercise has revealed to you about moving the relationship forward. That is the real challenge: to move from understanding to action.

7   The Community and the School

The term 'corporate life of the school' is often taken as a given and as such remains undefined and only partially understood. Ask a student teacher or perhaps even an experienced teacher 'What is the corporate life of the school?' and the answers can be multifarious:

- 'It's the ethos of the school';
- 'Is it the management?';
- 'I think it's to do with the financial management and leadership of the school';
- 'All the bits of school life that aren't the curriculum'; and
- 'Extra-curricular activities?'.

Indeed, it might seem that there are as many definitions of the term as there are teachers. So what then is the corporate life of the school?

This chapter will explore the term 'corporate life of the school' in order to both define and problematise it. The chapter will consider the role of the corporate life of the school in the socialisation of pupils by relating to historical and contemporary official educational policy and practice in order to develop an understanding of why schools are organised in the ways they are. It will also suggest ways in which you might contribute to the corporate life of your schools and gather evidence of meeting the brief Standard 1.5: 'They can contribute to, and share responsibly in, the corporate life of schools.'

A USEFUL METAPHOR

The TTA's *Qualifying to Teach: Handbook of Guidance* has this to say in relation to Standard 1.5:

> Schools are communities within which adults and pupils work together. The staff of the school as a whole need to work together to support

pupils' learning. Teachers contribute in a range of ways to a school's well-being and development. The school has a collective relationship with the community it serves. The communal nature of a school can teach pupils about how communities work and how interdependent individuals are.

(2003:10)

On closer inspection of this statement, key phrases in the paragraph appear to be '...adults and pupils work together', 'The staff...as a whole need to work together', 'collective relationship' and 'communal nature'. Certainly, one definition of the word 'corporate' is 'united' and the word itself has its origins in the Latin *corpus, corporis* – 'the body'. If we now think of the corporate life of the school as a united entity or 'body' how might an exploration of metaphorical language inform our understanding of the term?

To begin with the foundation of any vertebrate body, the *skeleton* might be the curriculum, pastoral system and other management structures upon which the body is built and which support the various activities of the body. The *nervous system* could be the agreed policies, procedures and communication systems within the school. The *lifeblood* of the body is the school's mission, the shared enterprise in the act of learning by pupils and their achievements in their daily lessons and in the learning and reflection by teachers through Continuing Professional Development. Within the *brain* would reside the collective knowledge, expertise and under-standings of all members of the corporate body. The *limbs* and *vital organs* would comprise all members of the body: governors, management team, teaching staff, administrative, technical and support staff, pupils, parents and other members of the community who have involvement with the school. In terms of *senses*, the school will have a *vision*; it will have a *voice* in the wider community it serves. In the way it deals with individuals and groups internally and externally it will have a palpable *touch*. It will have discernable *taste* in terms of its collective likes, dislikes, beliefs and values. Covering all and binding all of the foregoing together – the *skin*, as largest organ of the corporate body – is the ethos of the school.

The ethos of the school is of paramount importance. The term *ethos*, the Greek *custom, character*, refers to the habitual character and disposition of the school. It is, therefore, of moral significance and cannot be underestimated in any discussion of professional values. The ethos of the school is the tangible, as well as the abstract, manifestation of the common beliefs, values and dispositions of all members of the school. It is not untrue to say that the ethos of the school will not only be seen in all areas of the corporate life of the school, it also will be felt by pupils, staff and visitors.

When all parts of the corporate body are working to their fullest capacity, they contribute to its 'well-being and development' – the social, economic, political, educational and moral health of the school.

The corporate life of the school, then, is *everything* that goes on in a school on a day-to-day basis: teaching, learning, organisational structures, policies, the curriculum and interpersonal relationships. How do teachers treat pupils? How do pupils treat teachers? How do pupils treat each other? How do teachers treat each other? – and so on.

The corporate life of the school is also enshrined in its discourse, the language it uses to describe aspects of its work and the ways in which teachers use language with pupils. What are the different messages encapsulated in the following examples of language commonly used in contemporary school settings:

- 'dinner ladies' or 'midday supervisors'?
- 'premises officer' or 'caretaker'?
- a list of rules on a classroom wall, all of which begin 'Don't'?
- registers that list all the female pupils' names alphabetically before/after an alphabetical list of all male pupils' names?
- teachers referring to female pupils by their forenames and male pupils by the surnames?
- teachers, who in their teaching refer to their class as 'kids'?
- teachers who, when calling for attention in a mixed class, address male pupils as 'Chaps' or 'Guys' or 'Gentlemen' and female pupils as 'Girls'?

Language is important because it not only describes the corporate life in which it is located, it also creates and shapes that environment and its values and attitudes.

The corporate life of the school is reflected in, and exemplified by, the physical fabric of the environment: quality of displays, currency of notice boards, levels of graffiti and litter, quality and state of fabric, furnishings and decoration of buildings, the upkeep of any grounds surrounding the school and so on. How welcoming do visitors find the entrance and reception areas of the school? What messages does the school give to pupils about collective ownership of the buildings? A school policy that consigns all pupils to the playground during break or lunchtime – except when they are herded like damp cattle into a grossly overcrowded school hall during 'wet break' routine – and invokes sanctions and punishments on any pupil found inside, will do little to make pupils feel truly that they are regarded equally, or that they might have an equal part to play in the school's decision-making processes.

The corporate life of the school is a fundamental means of socialisation of pupils into the wider community outside their homes and ultimately contributes to their preparation for adult life. In recent years it has been given renewed emphasis through the introduction of Citizenship in the National Curriculum that emphasises the importance of pupils finding out about 'their rights and duties as individuals and members of communities' (QCA, 1999a: 136). However, state education has always had the combined roles of imparting knowledge, developing understandings and skills and socialising pupils based upon perceived future adult needs. The balance between individual needs and the perceived needs of society, or the nation, has varied over time and has led to the construction of subjects, curricula, schools and organisational systems along gender lines. It is most important to acknowledge that the corporate life of the school, therefore, is not a 'given'. It is a construct that has changed (and will continue to change) over time and it has been (and continues to be) subject to changing dominant educational, societal, economic and political discourses. It is useful, therefore, to briefly explore the changing approaches to the organisation of schools over the last half century in order to explore the structural issues related to the corporate life of the school.

SCHOOL ORGANISATION

The purpose of the 1944 Education Act was to regenerate the country and provide an education system that would develop all pupils to their fullest potential. The so-called Butler Act also made it the duty of all local authorities to contribute to the spiritual, moral, mental and physical development of the community. However, it could be seen that the establishment of a tripartite system of schooling comprising grammar, technical and modern schools was premised on beliefs about the development of aptitudes appropriate to future working lives and was one of the causes of underachievement of working-class children (Davison, 2000: 248) (see also Chapter 4 Expectations, Diversity and Achievement).

The tripartite system created very different corporate lives in the three types of schools. Many grammar schools, usually single-sex, with their emphasis on academic achievement perpetuated the corporate life and ethos of public schools with pastoral systems based on houses, streamed teaching groups, 'masters' or 'mistresses' in academic gowns, celebration of competition and sporting prowess, and so on. Technical schools, usually single-sex boys' schools, were aimed at preparing pupils for working lives in industry such as engineering, building. Consequently, the curricula in such establishments tended to comprise mathematics, science and craft-based subjects. At times, the ethos of such schools had all the allure of a poorly equipped factory floor, or a brickyard with books. Modern schools were the fate of everybody else that did not pass the eleven-plus and they focused on preparing young adults for work in commerce and trade, or through subjects like cookery and housecraft for girls' perceived future lives as wives and mothers. Many young adults left such schools without qualifications beyond typing and clerical certificates.

The advent of comprehensive schools posed new challenges for those charged with developing and managing the corporate life of institutions, many of which contained in excess of two thousand pupils. Comprehensive schools were not a product of the 1960s although that is when they expanded. The first purpose-built comprehensive school was opened in southeast London in 1954. In terms of making the management of large numbers of pupils possible, Kidbrooke School, like many later comprehensive schools, without the slightest hint of irony turned to the House System as the basis for its pastoral organisational means. Schools founded with egalitarian zeal upon notions of social justice and personal development chose a system that had its origins in the very antithesis of comprehensive schools, the elitist world of public schools.

The construction of pastoral systems founded upon the House System in both grammar and comprehensive schools clearly shows that state education is not only concerned with the academic development of pupils, but it is concerned with the development of the whole child, academically, intellectually, affectively, spiritually and morally. Such beliefs, of course, underpin the Personal, Social and Health Education and Citizenship curricula developed as part of the National Curriculum. Historically (and of course currently), pupils in independent schools would have boarded, slept, eaten and to some extent studied within houses, which were actual buildings in the grounds of the schools. It is argued that this system fostered a caring ethos that was concerned with the development of the whole individual. In 1800 the Headmaster (sic) of Christ's Hospital School, the Reverend Boyer stated 'The school is your father! Boy, the school is your mother...and all your relatives, too!' (Davison, 1998). The direct legacy of this historical organisation is found in the House Systems in many schools today, and in many ways it is a uniquely British phenomenon. While many schools today organise pastoral structures on an age-related Year System, many use the House System. And in some schools, they use a combination of both.

What are the aims of the organisation of the pastoral care system of your school? Do they match the general ethos of the school? What is the relationship if any between the management of behaviour and discipline in the school and the pastoral organisation? What is the general climate of the school and the nature of social relations? How does it feel to walk around the school – particularly on a first visit?

PUPIL INVOLVEMENT

In order to fulfil the aims of the 1944 Education Act, the Crowther Report (Ministry of Education, 1959) proposed that the school-leaving age should be raised to sixteen years (an innovation only achieved two decades later) and that the final year in the secondary modern school should be seen as a transition from school to the world of work. In relation to the curriculum for students in further education, the Report identifies four main curricular aims that enable young workers to find their way in the adult world, which include training for citizenship.

Other aims relate to moral values, education for leisure and vocational education. Lawton (1973: 108) is critical of the Report because it 'failed to make any real link between the excellent early chapters on social change and the later chapters on curriculum...Despite the extensive use of the Report by sociologists to support arguments about equality of opportunity, from the point of view of curriculum it is a very conservative, unimaginative document.'

In terms of a development in pupils of a sense of community, the 1963 Newsom Report offers two areas of focus: internal and external. The Report promotes the positive aspects of pupils' involvement in the community of the school through 'work or activities specifically communal in nature – a mural for the dining room, a lectern for the hall, curtains for the stage...providing refreshments for some social occasion' because 'the knowledge that they are contributing, and the public appreciation of their efforts, can strengthen morale of many of our boys and girls' (Ministry of Education, 1963: 131). It is clear that the Report moves beyond a consideration only of vocational preparation in order to serve the needs of society, the promotion of community service and the development of individual self-esteem. The chapter on *Spiritual and Moral Development* acknowledges the difficulties faced by schools where the values of the school may be at variance with the values of pupils' homes. The Report notes that within the 'difference of standard between the multiple worlds of which we are all citizens lies a limiting factor to what a school can do. Its influence may well be only temporary, having no carry-over, unless it succeeds in making clear to its members that the standards it sets, and often in large measure achieves, are just as relevant to the whole of life as to the part which is lived within its walls. There is no automatic transfer of values; boys and girls need to be convinced that what applies in school ought to apply to all human relations' (Ministry of Education, 1963: 53). The Report's four recommendations related spiritual and moral development, and each proposes the traditional benefits of well-structured Religious Education. It is interesting to note that in many current OFSTED reports – see the OFSTED Report Website http://www.ofsted.gov.uk/reports/ – the corporate act of daily worship is cited as a very positive building block in the corporate life of schools.

Lawton (1973) notes a change of attitude in the Newsom Report to the social education of pupils. 'Here is a slight ideological shift, moving away from elitist notions to ideals of social justice and equality' (Lawton, 1973: 109), which is in keeping with a general tendency for industrial societies to move away from an elitist view of society towards a more egalitarian view.

CITIZENSHIP AND THE CORPORATE LIFE OF THE SCHOOL

The National Curriculum documents Curriculum Guidance 7 *Environmental Education* (NCC, 1990a), and Curriculum Guidance 8 *Education for Citizenship*

(NCC, 1990b) also show a growing concern with the benefits of making a full contribution to the life of a community in relation to individual pupil needs. The 'guiding principles' of environmental education include 'the common duty of maintaining, protecting and improving the quality of the environment' and 'the way in which each individual, by his own behaviour, particularly as a consumer, contributes to the protection of the environment' (NCC, 1990a: 3). The personal and social skills listed in the document that can be developed through environmental education appear to be remarkably limited. The skills are 'working co-operatively with others, e.g. participating in group activities for the environment' and 'taking individual and group responsibility for the environment, e.g. for disposal of litter' (NCC, 1990a: 6). How far can a school justify a punishment of litter-picking in the playground as a positive contribution to the corporate life of the school and to the individual pupil's environmental education?

Attitudes that are thought to be developed through environmental education are appreciation, independence of thought, respect, tolerance and open-mindedness. Lawton (1973) neatly sums up the inadequacy of such an approach to education for social awareness: 'It is not simply educating for toleration, it also involves knowing what are the limits of toleration and where it may be necessary to stand firmly on one's principles. All of this is quite impossible without a high level of understanding, not only of politics and economics but also of what values are, why value systems are similar in some respects and different in others, what principles are involved in making values-judgements, and so on' (Lawton, 1973: 133).

How far then is, or indeed should be, making a full contribution to the corporate life of the school merely an acceptance of, and a perpetuation of, the status quo? Can a teacher make a full and valid contribution to the corporate life of the school by being at times *critical* of certain aspects of the corporate life of the school? How does a pupil make her or his voice heard about aspects of school life considered unjust? Does the critiquing of the corporate life of the school lead to anarchy or contribute to school improvement?

CONTEMPORARY ISSUES

Two decades ago, in *The Challenge for the Comprehensive School*, Hargreaves (1982: 34–35) lamented that schools lost their 'corporate vocabulary'. He believed that phrases such as 'team spirit', *'esprit de corps'* and 'loyalty to the school' had declined in favour of a culture of individualism. Hargreaves argues in favour of schools making a contribution to the social solidarity of society, which would be promoted by citizenship education based on experiential learning through community service. Integral to Hargreaves' model of a community-centred curriculum is the proposal of community studies, including practical community service. This version of a curriculum would comprise a core of 'traditional' subjects organised around community studies, with a reduction of the influence of external examinations in favour of increased school-based teacher assessment.

Arguably, the corporate life of the school reflects the political and social context within which it is constructed and educational legislation in the intervening two decades has constructed the National Curriculum that is, in many ways, the antithesis of Hargreaves' model of a community-centred curriculum. However, it is interesting to observe that with the re-election of a New Labour Government for a second term, such ideas have resurfaced and much of what Hargreaves proposes can be found in curricula-developing as a result of the Crick Report. This fact is, perhaps, unsurprising when we note that Professor Hargreaves is acknowledged in the Crick Report as having contributed to the work of the Advisory Group on Citizenship (QCA, 1998: 83).

A key feature of education for citizenship stated in the earlier publication on citizenship, Curriculum Guidance 8, is 'to strengthen the bond between the individual and community' (NCC, 1990b: 1). The curricular objectives of *Education for Citizenship* are knowledge, cross-curricular skills, attitudes, moral codes and values. Central to the first objective is development of knowledge and understanding of 'The nature of community' comprising: local and worldwide communities; how communities combine stability with change; the organisation of communities and the importance of rules and laws, and how communities reconcile the needs of the individual with those of society (NCC, 1990b: 3)

The document promotes the development of shared values 'such as concern for others, industry and effort, self-respect and self-discipline, as well as moral qualities such as honesty and truthfulness'. It also acknowledges that 'distinguishing between right and wrong is not always straightforward' because an 'individual's values, beliefs and moral codes change over time and are influenced by personal experience (e.g. of the family, friends, the media, school, religion) and the cultural background in which an individual is raised' (NCC, 1990b: 4). Much of what is proposed in relation to Key Stages 1–4 follows the 'traditional' model of information-gathering in core and foundation subjects and Personal, Social and Health Education (PSHE). The concept of service to the community is to be developed in pupils through 'a community or business enterprise' that is evaluated in terms of 'costs and benefits' (NCC, 1990b: 4). For a short time in the late 1980s and early 1990s, the corporate life of the school took on shades of the corporate life of Thatcherite free-market libertarianism with pupils engaged in 'mini-enterprises' aimed at making financial profit out of other pupils, teachers, parents and members of the wider community.

Both *National Curriculum for England* documents (Key Stages 1 and 2 (QCA, 1999a), Key Stages 3 and 4 (QCA, 1999b)) are premised upon a statement of values, aims and purposes (see for example QCA, 1999a: 10–12). In the preamble to the non-statutory guidelines for PSHE and Citizenship at Key Stages 1 and 2 the authors state the importance of pupils finding out about 'their rights and duties as individuals and members of communities' (QCA, 1999a: 136). Key Stage 3 indicates a shift towards more active community involvement: 'meet and work with people (e.g. people who can give them reliable information about health and safety issues, such as school nurses)'. The example continues by advocating that pupils should 'participate' and 'develop relationships' by working together in a range of groups. However, such activities comprise 'being responsible for a mini-enterprise scheme as part of a small group' (QCA, 1999b: 190) and are clearly a reworking of earlier ideas. Other recommendations refer to the traditional 'work experience and industry days' (QCA, 1999b: 193), and the announcement by the Secretary of State in the autumn of 2003 concerning the positive reasons of the reintroduction of vocational curricula in Key Stage 4 supports such recommendation. Despite the fact that the revised *National Curriculum for England* is for the first time predicated upon clearly articulated beliefs and values, there is much that is traditional in what is proposed in relation to personal, social and vocational development and the corporate lives of schools.

CONTRIBUTING TO THE CORPORATE LIFE OF THE SCHOOL

The TTA *Handbook of Guidance* (TTA, 2003) expects student teachers to 'develop an understanding of the ethos of the school...its sense of purpose and how it represents itself' (p. 10). The foregoing discussion of the evolution of the corporate life of the school should have provided you with sufficient background information to be able to ask not only the sorts of questions posed in this chapter, but also the ones that encapsulate your professional concerns as you develop as a reflective practitioner. You are also expected to 'seek to reflect and promote' the school's ethos and sense of purpose in your own teaching and to develop the ability to make a contribution to the corporate life of the school beyond your own classroom.

Some ways in which you might make such contribution are straightforward and develop almost naturally as part of your teaching: developing resources and materials to be shared across a year, or across the department; with an experienced colleague, sharing responsibility for the organisation and execution of an educational visit or field trip – if you are particularly fortunate, this might be a residential experience; participating in after-school activities such as literacy, numeracy or subject enrichment, homework club, library duty, or extra-curricular activities such as drama group, team sport coaching and so on. In a wider arena you might contribute to the organisation and running of open days/evenings, parent–teacher meetings. Attendance at parents evenings gives student teachers insights into the relationships between what teachers believe to be good practice in subject teaching and the expectations of parents, which may be based on their understanding of the presentation of the curriculum and other educational issues in the media.

Another way of becoming involved in the corporate life of the school is to make a contribution to the development of departmental or whole school policies. Davison and Dowson (2003) have this to say about the importance of department meetings:

> Departmental meetings are at the heart of a teacher's working life and are an excellent source for your own professional development. However, initially, they can appear daunting occasions. To be surrounded by confident, experienced subject specialists can make you all too aware of how little you really know about teaching the subject. However, you should attempt to make a contribution to the work of the department beyond your own classroom teaching. Good relationships with your departmental colleagues also mean sharing ideas and resources. It is important, therefore, for you to take as full a part as is appropriate in departmental discussions and decision-making. Many teachers, departments and schools engage in teacher education precisely because student teachers bring a new perspective and fresh ideas. You should display confidence (but not over confidence) in your knowledge and abilities, but also have a realistic awareness of your needs and the gaps in your knowledge and understanding, which are, for the most part, the result of the limited experience of teaching that you have had hitherto. Above all, you will be expected to ask questions. Such involvement will develop your understandings of how a department is managed; how a school curriculum emerges, and it will highlight the fact that teaching is always a matter of choices.
>
> (p. 293)

Engaging in the way suggested above will not only enable you to make a fuller contribution to the corporate life of the school, it will also enrich and deepen your understanding of it.

TASK   School Policy

While the thought of making a contribution to 'whole school policies' might feel enormously daunting, it is helpful to remember that although there may be large-scale discussion in a staff meeting about policy, much discussion and formulation goes on in department meetings or working parties. An attempt to draft policy with a group of 70+ members of staff sitting around a table is doomed from the start.

The examples below are based upon extracts of policy statements made by schools. As you read the extracts, consider the following questions:

1   How would you feel about working in these schools?
2   How far do the statements of policy reflect the Professional Values and Practices articulated in *Qualifying to Teach*?
3   What would you expect the ethos of the two schools to be like?

Extract A

Teachers will need to make a full contribution to the corporate life of the school. Therefore we will:

- Feel aligned and positive about the Vision, Values and Teaching Framework of the school and happy to share them with anyone interested;
- Work willingly and co-operatively with other teachers, share and be open to new ideas, aware of the skills of other teachers, and able to ask for help when needed;
- Be seen as a positive member of the teaching staff, participating in corporate activities;
- Feel confident to confront felt concerns (between any members of the school community) openly so that issues can be resolved in a creative manner;
- Make sure all school policies and procedures are adhered to; and
- Take every opportunity to gain professional development and be able to show evidence of the new ideas you have introduced into your class.

Extract B

Pupils will be expected to:

- learn and help others learn;
- think critically and creatively;
- develop intellectual integrity;
- be supportive of the beliefs, ideals and expectations of the school;
- strive to the best of their ability in all aspects of their schoolwork;
- take care of the school environment and their own belongings;
- display acceptable social skills/manners;
- be respectful;
- care for one another – support one another;

- take increased responsibility for their actions, learning, equipment and for the consequences of the choices they make;
- be proud of their individual cultural identity;
- respect other cultures; and
- show a sense of belonging and loyalty to the school.

Teachers will:

- be learners, foster in students the desire and drive for knowledge and learning;
- be committed to providing substantial and relevant learning experiences;
- be committed to developing thinking strategies and problem-solving skills in students;
- be committed to developing independent lifelong learners;
- demonstrate loyalty and commitment to the management, governors, staff and culture of the school;
- be caring;
- work as a team;
- create environments that: promote learning, are bright, are irresistible, thought provoking and challenging;
- be professional, informed and committed; and
- value diversity.

CONCLUSION

All bodies need sustenance. All bodies go through a continuing process of renewal. The corporate life and therefore the ethos of the school reflects the collective values, aspirations, hopes, desires and beliefs not only about teaching and learning, but also about what it means to be part of a human community that lives and grows together on a daily basis. The central focus of your contribution to the corporate life of the school must be about making a positive contribution to the dynamic community that is the school. Your wider involvement in the life of the school should never be reduced to ticking off a list of evidence for your professional development portfolio – cynical, hollow approaches are soon unmasked.

At times it may be difficult to support all policies and practices you find in operation in a placement school. Such dilemmas are exacerbated, of course, because you may have been placed in a school in which you might not necessarily choose to work as an NQT. It may be a matter of complete indifference to you if a pupil in your class has not: worn the correct shoes, tucked in a shirt, etc., but if there is a policy as 'Extract A' above notes, teachers need to 'Make sure all school policies and procedures are adhered to', not out of a Draconian sense of conformity, but out of a sense of consistency, pupils will not thank you for being inconsistent. Essentially the way to deal with any unease that you might feel is recommended in 'Extract A' above. After noting a concern in your *Reflective Journal* (see Chapter 8) you should discuss matters with your mentor/tutor 'openly so that issues can be resolved in a creative manner'.

It is interesting to note, and hopefully it was comforting to recognise, that many of points expressed in the examples of school policies above were very similar indeed to the Professional Values and Practices in *Qualifying to Teach*. It is equally interesting to note that neither policy quoted above as 'Extract A' and 'Extract B' came from a school in the United Kingdom.

8 Personal and Professional Development

The TTA's *Handbook of Guidance* (2003) is quite clear about the benefits of reflective practice:

> To teach effectively, teachers need to have the capacity and commitment to analyse and reflect on their own practice, and to improve it throughout their careers through professional development and engagement with new knowledge and ideas.

This chapter addresses Standard 1.7 'They are able to improve their own teaching, by evaluating it, learning from the effective practice of others and from evidence. They are motivated and able to take increasing responsibility for their own professional development' and considers the development of critical reflection that will enable you to build upon, and to develop, personal theories of teaching that can be articulated and translated into practice through the synthesis of experiences gained during the ITE course. The chapter will also explore ways of 'reading' effective practice of experienced teachers through the practice of discursive mentoring. It will also consider the establishment of processes and practices that will be the foundation of ongoing professional development from NQT through the early years of teaching. You will find it useful to refer back to Chapter 3 'Professional Values in the Classroom' when we come to consider planning and evaluation of lessons later in this chapter. Similarly, Standard 3.1.2 in the *Handbook* provides a useful overview of planning and evaluation of lessons.

The language that surrounds and defines the practices and processes of teacher education is an example of 'communication in an institutionalised socio-cultural context' (Bhatia, 1995: 4). During the last decade, the discourse of teacher education has been to a large extent shaped by the language of government circulars. With DES Circular 9/92 the term 'competence' became central to the language of teacher education and subsequently, Circulars 4/98 and 02/02 have promoted a 'Standards-based' model of initial teacher preparation. Nevertheless, other terminology of widely differing meaning, such as 'apprenticeship' and 'reflective practice' have also been prevalent. On the one hand, teacher development might be characterised as the acquisition of skills and content, while on the other hand, it is argued that teacher development is concerned with developing the processes of critical thinking as a reflective practitioner. It is common to find in official documents and texts on teacher development the terms teacher education and teacher training used as if they are interchangeable. However, *education* and *training* are two very different processes, each of which might imply the user's underlying conception of teacher development. The establishment of a TTA rather than a Teacher Education Agency perhaps has more to do with beliefs about the nature of teaching and how that 'craft' might best be learned, rather than a concern about acronyms.

Roses and fruit trees are *trained* to grow in externally pre-determined ways. Seals are *trained* to perform set routines repeatedly without error. German Shepherd dogs are *trained* to respond immediately, in precise ways to given stimuli. While it cannot be denied that there are particular skills that might be developed through training and practice, teachers should be not only trained, they should be *educated*. Working in school requires the need to exercise judgement related to teaching and learning that will be a synthesis of experience, skills, knowledge, understandings, values and beliefs anchored in the field of educational discourses. This synthesis of experience is the product of critical reflection upon practice and not of training alone.

Perhaps unsurprisingly, the reflective police dog has yet to be encountered.

STUDENT TEACHER DEVELOPMENT

> During their training, trainees can be expected to use the feedback they receive from more experienced colleagues observing their teaching, and their experience of observing others, to identify ways of improving their practice.
>
> (TTA, 2003)

Student teacher development is not a narrow linear progression, nor the climbing of a ladder of hierarchical stages of teacher competence from novice to the zenith of advanced skills teacher. Rather it results from a complex web of interactions that take place between the individual, the teacher education programme, the school context, fellow student teachers, mentors, pupils and tutors. Furthermore, each student teacher begins a course with a range of experiences, values, attitudes, knowledge, understanding, skills, qualities and needs. Student teacher development is far more complex than even *Qualifying to Teach* (TTA, 2002) would have us believe and in many ways it is unique to the individual.

Perhaps a useful analogy for the process is to think of student teacher development as taking place in the same way that a photographer develops a photograph in a developing tray. The photographic image does not develop uniformly from nothing: at one moment a blank sheet; the next a fully formed, crystal-clear picture. Instead, as the image swims into view, different parts of it emerge simultaneously and independently: a highlight here, a fragment of landscape there, a detail of shadow, now a facial feature, until the complete image emerges. What emerges first and last depends on interactions between information stored in the paper and the chemicals acting upon it. Similarly, the development of the student teacher's practice, knowledge, understandings and beliefs is a synthesis of experiences. In the classroom context it may be some time before a 'complete' picture of teaching emerges. Indeed, it may take many years.

The process of synthesising enables student teachers to focus, probe, test and begin to make sense of emergent classroom images. Information that student teachers use in this process may come from two main sources. The first source may be direct experience through observation or teaching in the classroom. The second source may be a result of reading, writing or discussion with a range of people. Indeed, it is most likely that student teachers will draw from combinations of many sources. Student teacher development is complex, because teaching is a complex process, which goes far beyond 'delivering' a curriculum.

REFLECTIVE PRACTICE

During the last decade, the terms *reflection* and the development of the *reflective practitioner* (Schön, 1983; Calderhead, 1989; Rudduck, 1991; Jalongo and Isenberg, 1995; Arthur *et al.*, 1997) have become central to any discussion of teacher development. Indeed, it would appear that the reflective practitioner is 'the dominant model of professional in teacher education' (Whiting *et al.*, 1996).

Calderhead (1989) provides a useful overview of the definitions of reflection that have emerged in the writing related to teaching and teacher education. To varying degrees, reflective practice is seen to incorporate *inter alia* a variety of features including:

- problem setting and solving;
- the development of analytical skills and attitudes that facilitate reflection, such as self-awareness and self-determination; and
- the examination of values, moral principles and ideological and institutional constraints.

Such features encompass, and are the foundation of, the *process, content, pre-conditions* and *product* of reflection. Korthagen and Wubbels (1995: 55) sum up reflection as 'the mental process of structuring or restructuring an experience, a problem or existing knowledge or insights'.

It is not possible in a chapter of this length fully to explore the nature and scope of reflection, but McLaughlin (1994: 6–13) usefully locates conceptions of reflection along two continua. The first continuum refers to the *nature* of reflection. At one end are versions of reflection that stress the 'explicit and systematic' (cf. Dewey, 1933); at the other end, the 'implicit and intuitive' (Schön, 1983). The second continuum concerns itself with the *scope* and *objects* of reflection:

> One way of describing the continuum on which the scope and objects of reflection are located is in terms of a concern at one end of the continuum for specific and proximate matters and a concern at the other for matters which are general and contextual.
>
> (McLaughlin, 1994: 12)

McIntyre (1993) identifies three levels of reflection which are embedded in the Oxford Internship scheme:

- the *technical* level – concerned with the attainment of goals;
- the *practical* level – concerned with the 'assumptions, predispositions, values and consequences with which actions are linked'; and
- the *critical* or *emancipatory* level.

In the final level, concern ranges to wider social, political and ethical issues which include 'the institutional and societal forces which may constrain the individual's freedom of action or limit the efficacy of his or her actions' (McIntyre, 1993: 44).

This structuring draws on Carr and Kemmis's (1986) work with categories derived from Habermas (1974). While such categorisation may help to clarify thinking about reflection in an attempt to articulate teacher development, there is the danger that the implied hierarchy of these three levels can lead us to believe that reflection at the *practical* level is inferior to *critical* reflection (see Griffiths and Tann, 1992).

PURPOSES OF REFLECTION

If we accept that different levels of reflection can be identified, we must also acknowledge that student teachers will engage in reflection in different ways, at different times, for different reasons. Frost (1993: 140) summarises the *purposes* of reflection and how the process enables the student teacher to:

- assess his or her own skills and to improve them;
- evaluate the chosen teaching strategies and materials in terms of their appropriateness;
- question the values embedded in those practices and proceed to challenge the aims and goals for teacher education;
- continue to examine and clarify their personal values and beliefs about society and pedagogy;
- theorise about the context of their pedagogical practice – that is, to try to develop explanations about the pupils, the interactions in the classroom and about the processes of teaching and learning; and
- examine the adequacy of theories about pedagogical contexts and processes and develop a critique of them.

Reflective practice is a process that enables a student teacher to develop classroom practice in the short term, and also begins the development of habitual reflection that subsequently enables the teacher to continue to improve practice throughout his or her career. To elaborate: structured, guided reflection on, or analysis of, a student teacher's own practice, in the light of required reading, or school-based investigations that are part of an ITE course, will begin to develop initial competence in the context of a particular school-experience classroom. This experience will also develop practices of reflection, supported by the *Career Entry and Development Profile*, which NQTs may use in whatever school context they find themselves subsequently. Indeed, they may continue to use these practices during their careers to facilitate their professional development.

On many ITE programmes, in the early stages of school experience, student teachers carry out systematic enquiry into aspects related to their own practice. The exact focus may be chosen by the student teacher, usually in discussion with tutor and/or mentor, in order to meet a perceived need, or to make visible some aspect of practice, which is as yet unclear to them. Calderhead has criticised student teachers' ability to reflect, describing it as 'shallow' (Calderhead, 1987: 277) because these early reflection activities tend, in the main, to be *descriptive* in nature rather than *reflective*. However, this fact should not surprise us, nor does it invalidate or diminish the activity; for it is in the initial stages, in such *articulation* or *description* of some aspect of practice that may seem blindingly obvious to the experienced teacher, that learning and development take place. Description in these early stages can for the first time make visible the processes of teaching: make visible the elements of experienced teachers' practice that for student teachers appear a seamless flow.

Early articulation or description of the practice of others can allow student teachers to begin to probe his or her own personal theories of teaching and learning: the theories and images of teaching and learning which they bring to the teacher education course. Griffiths and Tann (1992) propose that we should not view reflection as hierarchical, privileging so-called critical reflection over practical reflection (McIntyre, 1993), rather all student teachers and teachers, who might be considered to be reflective, should engage in all levels in their careers. Therefore a student teacher, or, indeed, an experienced teacher, might engage in the form of reflective practice most appropriate to the context in which they find themselves. In such a manner 'small scale and particular' *personal* theories, which some might characterise as 'common sense', may be tested against and informed by 'large scale and universal' *public* theories:

> Everyone has to start somewhere, and no-one can start everywhere. It is being argued that all of the levels are an essential part of reflective practice. At any one time the focus may be on one or another of them, but it is vital that each reflective practitioner should follow all of them at some time.
>
> (Griffiths and Tann, 1992: 79)

Even though the number of Standards has been reduced in recent years, it is a daunting prospect to be confronted by fifty-plus Standards in the cold type of *Qualifying to Teach*. Unfortunately there are no easy answers to the questions 'how well am I doing?', 'will I make a good teacher?' What can be said is that you are not expected to demonstrate or achieve all the Standards all at once. If you are unsure about your ability to 'make it' as a teacher, what will be looked for is evidence of progress. Progress will be made, and more significantly, measured, through a process of setting specific targets and, through reflection, identifying achievements and areas for development. A survey by HMI noted differences in the ways student teachers viewed school experience. Some NQTs looked back on their school experience as a time of testing and conformity rather than a period of experimentation and growth. Conversely, many NQTs had appreciated being able to make mistakes and learn from them:

> The teachers particularly valued having a wide range of classes and an opportunity to observe experienced teachers.... 'It was a vital part of training. I had to try out ideas, make mistakes, discover weaknesses in myself and start again.'
>
> (OFSTED, 1993: 4.27)

The processes of realistic self-appraisal and target-setting will not happen in isolation. This early professional development will be done in conjunction with other student teachers, class teachers, the head of department, tutors and above all, with mentors, through specific, constructive verbal and written feedback.

INITIAL REFLECTIONS

The process of developing as a reflective practitioner is highly likely to begin within days of commencing your ITE course. Indeed, it may even begin before you begin the course. It is important to benchmark a student teacher's current knowledge, skills and understandings and to determine the main areas for professional development. Therefore, many student teachers are required to undertake a subject knowledge audit in relation to their degree and the National Curriculum subject in which they are intending to become a specialist.

Task   Subject Knowledge Audit

Obtain a copy of the National Curriculum for the age phase in which you are intending to teach and for the subject in which you intend to specialise. Usually, a copy of the National Curriculum will be supplied by your ITE provider, but you may also obtain an electronic version of it from the website *National Curriculum Online*: http://www.nc.uk.net/index.html. Examine the content of the subject and considering your previous education – degree content, A levels, GCSE subjects, other qualifications and experience – begin to create a table of five columns under the following headings:

Subject area	Confident	Not Confident	Action	Review date

The completion of this table will be the beginning of your professional development as a teacher. Do not be daunted by the growing 'Not Confident' column. Remember, one of the main purposes of your course is to enable you to develop knowledge and understanding of the National Curriculum. Conversely, it is wise not to be over-confident about your subject knowledge as there is a world of difference between many degree courses in English, for example, and National Curriculum English. Similarly, a major aim of your development will be to turn your subject knowledge into subject application in the classroom. Your *Subject Knowledge Audit* can be reviewed at key times throughout your course. It can form the basis of your action planning during your initial preparation and contribute to your *Career Entry and Development Profile* that you will take with you into your early years of teaching.

Berliner (1994) claims to be able to identify clear stages in the development of teacher expertise. His proposition is drawn from similarities that he believes are exhibited by experts in a range of areas including chess, nursing, football, air-traffic control and racehorse handicapping. Berliner proposes five stages through which the teacher journeys:

> We begin with the greenhorn, the raw recruit, the *novice*. Student teachers and many first-year teachers may be considered novices.

As experience is gained, the novice becomes an *advanced beginner*. Many second- and third-year teachers are likely to be in this developmental stage. With further experience and some motivation to succeed, the advanced beginner becomes a *competent* performer. It is likely that many third- and fourth-year teachers, as well as some more-experienced teachers, are at this level. At about the fifth year, a modest number of teachers may move into the *proficient* stage. Finally, a small number of these will move on to the last stage of development – that of *expert* teacher.

(Berliner, 1994: 108)

Berliner admits that the developmental sequence involved in the progression from novice to expert 'is not as yet clearly described'. However, his description of the novice seems overly simplistic. It ignores not only the diversity of entrants to teacher education courses, but also the range of knowledge, experience and expertise they bring with them. While some entrants to PGCE courses may be newly graduated twenty-one year olds, equally, a PGCE student teacher may be the PhD research chemist with twenty years' work experience in industry; the single parent in his early thirties with a master's degree; the Benedictine brother; the EFL teacher who has spent twenty-five years teaching in Europe and the middle east; the mother of grown-up children returning to teaching; the former police officer; and anyone with any other experience. While such student teachers might not have the characteristics of one of Berliner's *expert* teachers, each brings unique and diverse knowledge, experience and expertise.

Furlong and Maynard (1995) propose five broad stages of development that student teachers undergo during school experience. These stages are: 'early idealism', 'personal survival', 'dealing with difficulties', 'hitting a plateau' and 'moving on'. Furlong and Maynard are emphatic that these stages are not 'discrete or fixed; rather, they are...interrelated and mutable' (Furlong and Maynard, 1995: 73). In relation to new entrants to teacher education programmes, Furlong and Maynard (1995: 182) observe, it is 'important to recognise that no student teacher enters the classroom as a complete novice – they bring with them a vast array of skills, knowledge and understandings derived from other contexts.' Beyond the *Subject Knowledge Audit*, then, how might such diverse experience be captured?

INITIAL STATEMENT

As well as benchmarking subject knowledge and expertise, many teacher education programmes ask student teachers to give their reasons for coming into teaching. Such an exercise enables the student teacher to begin to examine their beliefs and

values in relation to teaching: beliefs and values that will underpin their work in the classroom and their development of reflective practice. Often student teachers are also asked to describe what they believe to be the skills, qualities and attributes of a good teacher.

At first sight their reasons appear many and various. However, after analysis it is clear that these reasons may be quite readily placed into a very few groups. In their *Initial Statements* the majority of student teachers write about 'love of subject', 'enthusiasm'; 'empathy', 'a desire to share the love of subject' and, indeed, 'to be of service' to others.

The following examples written by student teachers illustrate this point:

> 'My main reason for teaching stems from my love of the subject I wish to teach';
>
> 'I hope my enthusiasm for maths can be passed on as part of my teaching';
>
> 'If I can inspire pupils to be amazed by what a fantastic world they are part of, to enjoy their lives no matter what they are or become, then I might start considering myself as a teacher';
>
> 'I am looking forward to being able to pass on my love and enthusiasm for my subject';
>
> 'I think that perhaps the most important attributes are enthusiasm and energy. These qualities are needed to inspire pupils and get them all involved';
>
> 'I want to be the kind of teacher who can communicate my love of music to a class and instil in them a love of the subject';
>
> 'I believe a fundamental commitment to education is one of the most important things we can have as an individual and as a society;
>
> 'I have discovered what enormous pleasure can be drawn from sharing my own enthusiasm for learning and from making a valuable contribution to an individual's education and future'; and
>
> 'Studying for my degree has served to enhance my deep feeling of the privilege of learning and the duty to pass on knowledge. I feel a sense of joy in contributing to a child's success'.

Such statements exemplify Kelly's assertion that education is both a 'moral and a practical imperative in a democratic society' (see Chapter 1).

Clearly, the essence of these statements relates to notions of 'enthusiasm', 'love' and 'service'. All of them are founded upon strongly held beliefs and values. Teaching is, of course, a value-laden activity.

Perhaps, it would be too easy and indeed too cynical for experienced teachers to write off the foregoing students' statements as 'naïve' or 'idealistic'. Indeed, some academics have described the first stage of student teacher development as 'early idealism' (Furlong and Maynard, 1995). If we accept that the first stage of teacher development is characterised by 'early idealism', it is most important for us to clarify precisely what this term means. 'Idealism' has a number of meanings that are both positive and negative. The word can mean:

- love for, or search after, the best;
- impracticality; and
- the imaginative treatment of subjects.

Clearly, *idealism* can be equated with *impracticality*. However, early idealism is linked much more positively to the important personal and potentially professional values student teachers bring to initial teacher education.

The task of teacher educators is to help dispel any *illusions* about teaching that student teachers may bring to teacher education courses. At the same time, initial teacher preparation should enable NQTs to keep hold of, and indeed develop further, the idealism, the love, enthusiasm and desire to be of service that brings them into teaching in the first place. These are the very qualities that will sustain NQTs during the difficulties they will certainly encounter during their early careers. The real rewards of teaching are not monetary: they relate to teachers' self-esteem, which is enhanced by the sense of being valued in society for the wider, less tangible aspects of their role. Without enthusiasm, love and idealism, it is difficult for a teacher to sustain motivation and commitment.

TASK   Individual Statement

It is highly likely that you will have found that the student teachers on your course have had a variety of experiences before they embarked upon a teacher education course: some may be newly graduated in their early twenties, while others may have also studied for a higher degree; some may have had some teaching experience in the UK or abroad; others may have raised families or be embarking upon a second career. Whatever your and their experience has been, it is clear that you all have different kinds of knowledge and expertise that you will bring to your teaching. Equally, it is important that you are clear in your own mind about your own reasons for teaching. Using the headings given below, write an account of yourself. This will serve as a benchmark against which you will be able to gauge your development at strategic points of your course. When you have completed it, you might wish to share its contents with another student teacher, your tutor or mentor. Keep your *Individual Statement* as it will be useful at any stage during the year when you come to review your development. Once again, this will be one of the foundations for your development as a reflective practitioner.

Write an account of yourself using the following headings:

Stage of the course
Note the date so that you can monitor development since an earlier point or at a later point of the course.

Reasons for wanting to teach
Describe why/how you have decided to become a teacher.

Me as teacher
What sort of teacher do you wish to become? How would you like to be seen by pupils and colleagues?

Previous experience
Describe any experience you feel is relevant to the course, or to your intended career as a teacher.

Personal skills and qualities
Describe any qualities and skills you have that you believe to be appropriate to teaching.

Attitude to the subject
Describe any beliefs or principles you hold about the nature and importance of your own subject specialism as a school subject.

Professional concerns
Describe any current issues or problems you are concerned about in relation to teaching.

Any other issues

The TTA *Handbook of Guidance* (2003) reminds us that reflective practitioners seek out opportunities to review their own performance. The account you provide here will be an invaluable source of reflection at any later stage in the course and in your career. Will you regard these early statements as naïvely idealistic, or will they encapsulate fundamental principles that remain central to your educational philosophy? Only time will tell.

PLANNING

The *Handbook of Guidance* (TTA, 2003) is also clear about where some of the evidence will be found for student teachers' development in relation to Standard 1.8. 'Assessors will draw on trainee teachers' planning, and observations of their teaching, personal, action plans and reports of school-based tutors'. Similarly, the *Handbook* maintains that student teachers' lesson evaluations and other self-evaluations are likely to be especially useful in relation to this Standard.

Research by Tickle (1996) indicates that student teachers reflect mainly on the technicalities of teaching performance, which is focused on problem-solving and developing strategies which 'work' in the classroom (cf. McIntyre's (1993) 'technical level' of reflection, above). He found that aims and values underlying practice barely entered the realms of reflective consciousness, let alone becoming subject to any scrutiny and critique. Again, these findings should not surprise us. Much of the focus of early parts of a teacher education programme are aimed at developing a repertoire of skills that will enable student teachers to stand up in front of a group of pupils and do something useful. The focus of the student teacher is very much upon 'Me As Teacher' over a focus on pupil learning, which tends to characterise a slightly later stage of most courses and student teacher development. In relation to planning, therefore, the predominant interest is upon such aspects as content, pupil management, activities, resources, etc. If planning remains at this technical level, a teacher may become technically competent, but not become reflective. Focusing only upon 'what works', upon 'tips for teachers', might produce competent lessons, but it will not produce reflective practitioners who are able to engage in, and take responsibility for, their own professional development. This is where the Six Ws are helpful.

The Six Ws

The use of the Six Ws can be a means of beginning to develop reflective practice. Quite simply they are:

1   Who?
2   When?
3   Where?
4   What?
5   How?
6   Why?

It needs to be acknowledged from the outset that the list comprises five Ws and one H. However, it has more credibility than the Three Rs that are fully embedded in educational discourse, which after all comprise one R, one W and one A. The Six Ws are drawn from the world of journalism, where they are believed to form the basis of any story. However, for our purposes they serve as a ready checklist that will enable you to develop the practice of regular, habitual reflection that is a prerequisite of reflective practice and professional development.

The Six Ws may be applied not only to the planning of lessons, sequences of lessons or schemes of work, but also to evaluation of your own teaching, to your observation of your mentor's lessons and those of other colleagues. They are fundamental to self-review, to action planning and to successful personal and professional development. And the most important of the Ws is the sixth: 'Why?'. The first five Ws might be said to be located in the 'technical' level, but the application of the sixth W can help to move consideration of practice into the 'practical' and 'critical' levels.

In your early days in school, after a period of focused observation of your mentor or other experienced colleagues (to which we shall return shortly), you are likely to begin by taking responsibility for a part or parts of a lesson. Even when you begin to teach whole classes, much of the planning might have been done for you. Your answers to the six questions might look as follows:

1	Who	–	7DV
2	When	–	Monday Period 4 2.20–3.20 pm
3	Where	–	Room 212
4	What	–	Similes and Metaphors
5	How	–	Cloze procedure, pairs, electronic whiteboard work
6	Why	–	Departmental syllabus for Weeks 3–5.

While these answers may enable you to begin to plan how you might approach the lesson, they do not take us very far in developing reflective practice. The importance of the sixth W, 'Why?' lies in the fact that it should be applied to each of the five preceding Ws in order to spur further questions that will deepen your understanding of the contexts in which the lesson is taking place. The contexts may be school specific, but they may also be related to the wider social, political and economic contexts of teaching and learning.

1   Who – 7DV. Why am I being given a Year 7 class to teach early in my placement in school and not a Year 9, 11 or 13? Why this particular class? What should I know about particular needs of individual pupils?

2   When – Period 4. Why this time of day? How might it affect the choice of content, activity? How might it have affected the choice of class my mentor gave me?

3   Where – Room 212. Why this particular room? Has it anything to do with the way Year 7 are taught? In base rooms for core subjects? Was the choice of room determined by the nature of activity in which the class will engage? Did the fact that this is the only classroom in the English Department with an electronic whiteboard determine the activity? Why does the English Department have only one classroom with an electronic whiteboard, while the Science Department has six? What does this tell me

about the hierarchy of academic credibility of subjects in the school? What might it tell me about the relative funding of subjects in the school? Why is the National Curriculum built upon core and foundation subjects? What does this tell me about the hierarchy of academic credibility of subjects in the National Curriculum?

4   What – Similes and Metaphors. Why this particular aspect of the curriculum? Why are similes and metaphors considered important in the English curriculum? Why is this lesson placed at this point in the scheme of work? How does this lesson relate to previous pupil learning?

5   How – Cloze procedure, pairs, electronic whiteboard work. Why this particular way of delivery? What is the importance of pair work? What opportunities are there for assessment? What form might this take?

6   Why – Departmental syllabus for Weeks 3–5. Why is there an agreed Departmental syllabus, when there is a National Curriculum? How did it come about? Why cannot English teachers just teach what they want to do?, etc., etc.

These are just some of the many questions that might be asked. It might appear that such an approach leads to an infinite regression that ultimately stultifies and prevents a teacher from doing anything. This, of course, is not the case, as many of the answers that are at first novel become part of the working professional knowledge of the teacher. Planning your lessons, then, while being mindful of the Six Ws will enable you to begin to develop the habits of reflective practice. Within a very short time, the process will become second nature.

Furthermore, the process of visualisation has also been found to be useful in lesson preparation and planning. It is well documented that elite athletes use visualisation in order to rehearse performance and, indeed, to improve performance in a variety of sports. Similarly, experienced reflective teachers develop the capacity to visualise a lesson and to run through it in their heads – sometimes 'fast-forwarding' sections, or 'replaying' a section as a result of a 'What if?' question, perhaps in relation to common pupil misconceptions. Using and developing the ability to visualise the lessons you are about to teach will not only improve the quality of your planning and preparation, it will also quickly move you away from a dependence on the lesson plan that is sometimes clutched by beginning teachers as part script, part life preserver, part talisman.

EVALUATION

As noted earlier the *Handbook of Guidance* (TTA, 2003) maintains that student teachers' lesson evaluations and other self-evaluations are likely to be especially useful in relation to this Standard. Remember, the process of evaluation is not only summative, a kind of Wordsworthian 'emotion recalled in tranquility', but it is also a dynamic, ongoing, in-lesson process (see *Observation* below). It is well documented in such publications as the Hay McBer Report, Brown and Wragg's (1993) *Questioning*, or the TTA/Education Broadcasting Services Trust CDRom *Questions* (TTA, 2004) that central to formative, oral evaluation in a lesson is skillful questioning and answer sessions in the lesson. Good questioning technique is another key facet of your reflective practice repertoire.

Post-lesson evaluation should be equally dynamic. However, it is perhaps understandable that sometimes student teachers regard the written evaluation of lessons as a mechanical, externally imposed chore. However, in order that pupils make good progress and that you make progress as a beginning teacher, it is extremely important that you evaluate your lessons thoroughly. Your initial preparation programme will have its own specific requirements, therefore it would be inappropriate in this chapter to determine the exact number of evaluations that you might undertake during your school experience. What is important, however, is the nature of the evaluation and that it is undertaken on a regular basis whatever the frequency.

A weak lesson evaluation comes in many forms:

> 'Lesson went well today. All well behaved. Got through all material. They seem to understand the life cycle of the butterfly.'
> 'Ran out of time. Those boys were silly again. The class didn't seem too sure about Heisenberg's *Uncertainty Principle*.'
> 'A complete disaster. Class completely unruly. Hardly covered what I had planned to do. Will talk to Ms Heath about what to do next week.'

While these exact examples are fictional, they are not too dissimilar from evaluations to be found in professional development portfolios of some student teachers. The common factor is that they are wholly descriptive rather than analytical or reflective. They do not in any way recognise what the pupils have learned or partly learned, what were the causes of success or failure, what the teacher and pupils need to do next. Granted, in the third example the student teacher plans to meet with the mentor, but what will they discuss? However, this example does not consider pupil learning and in the first two examples comments on pupil learning are mere assertions. How does the student teacher know what the class has learned or not learned, what evidence is there for learning or otherwise?

Once again, the resolution to these difficulties lies in the questions that a teacher applies to post-lesson evaluation:

1   What happened/did not happen? Why?
2   What might be some of the reasons for success/lack of success? Are they issues to do with me, the pupils, the time of day, the preceding lesson that

the pupils had, the classroom, the content, the pupils' attitude to the topic/subject, the weather, and so on?

3   How might the factors pertaining to 1 and 2 be mitigated in future?

4   What more do I need to know about the subject, the topic, the class, classroom management, behaviour management, gender issues, learning styles, inclusion, pedagogy?

5   What additional/different materials and resources might I have used? Could information/resources/materials available from National Grid for Learning, publications from subject specialist/phase associations, research and inspection reports improve a lesson like this?

6   What did the pupils learn? How do I know? Where will I find the evidence?

7   What do I/the pupils need to do, know and understand before the next planned lesson?

8   How does what I've learned from teaching this lesson affect what I've planned to do in the next lesson in this sequence?

9   How does what I've learned from teaching this lesson contribute to my knowledge and understanding of the craft of teaching?

10   How does what I've learned from teaching this lesson affect how I might teach any lesson in the future?

This list is by no means exhaustive, but it does suggest the multiplicity of questions that need to be answered if truly reflective evaluation is to take place. The key point to remember about evaluation is that its importance lies in the fact that it is a *process* far more than it is a product that is used to fill your professional development portfolio.

OBSERVATION

The series of questions that teachers ask themselves become part of an internalised, silent dialogue that happens in experienced teachers' heads when lessons are being planned and, indeed, when a teacher is teaching a lesson. It is precisely this fact that makes it so hard for somebody new to the classroom to see 'how the teacher is doing it'. Like airline pilots, who do not wait until an aircraft is within a matter of feet above the ground before taking evasive action, all the time experienced teachers are teaching they are making a number of minor adjustments, calculating subtle actions or reactions that will ensure the success of the lesson. Arthur *et al.* (1997) explore this facet of teaching proposing that experienced teachers are able to teach successfully in this way because they engage in a dialogue with educational discourses.

Much has been written and much will be taught to you about the processes of observing your mentor and other experienced colleagues in the classroom. There is not space in this chapter to explore observation. It would be useful to you to consider some of the key texts relating to classroom practice such as Capel *et al.* (2003) *Learning to Teach in the Secondary School 3rd Edition* and the Hay McBer Report.

From what has gone before, it should be clear now that observation in the classroom is not a passive activity. Rather, as you watch experienced colleagues, you should be asking yourself the kinds of questions cited above and compare them with what you are beginning to learn and understand about teaching. Where you need clarification of a teacher's actions, note your questions and these can become the basis of the post-observation discussion. You will find that this is how your mentor will construct the agenda for debriefings of observations of you.

REFLECTIVE JOURNAL

Finally, how might you articulate your developing skills, knowledge and under-standings to help to provide you with a holistic view of your development as a beginning teacher? Many teachers, beginning and experienced, find a *Reflective Journal* invaluable in developing as a reflective practitioner. Indeed, a number of ITE programmes either use a journal or diary as an element of the developmental process during initial teacher preparation.

It must be emphasised, as is the case with evaluation, that the journal is not the 'Dear Diary' type of construction immortalised by Peter Cook's E.L. Wisty:

> *Monday*
> Got up. Went to the toilet. Sat in the park. Had lunch. Sat in the park. Went home. Tea. Went to bed.
>
> *Tuesday*
> Got up. Went to the toilet. Sat in the park. Had lunch. Sat in the park. Went home. Tea. Went to bed.
>
> *Wednesday*
> Got up. Sat in the park. Had lunch. Sat in the park. Went home. Tea. Went to bed. Didn't even go to the toilet.

The descriptive listing of your actions during school experience will not, by itself, enable you to develop as a reflective practitioner. However, journal entries are not another version of the lesson evaluations that you are also undertaking. The frequency of journal entries will be variable. Some programmes may have a specific weekly requirement, but the importance is that entries are regular and meaningful.

Entries are not necessarily accounts of Damascene revelations, although on occasion, they might be when you have particular successes. Your journal is a place in which you can pose questions about your developing understanding of practice – 'Why is it that Year 5 pupils cannot grasp...?' 'How can I make X more accessible?', etc.

As you go through your course the journal not only allows you to ask questions, to note significant developments and challenges, it also provides an excellent source for reflection. Visiting early journal entries at the end of your first period of school experience will enable you to appreciate the journey you have begun to make. Revisiting during your second school experience, towards the end of your course, or indeed as an NQT again will enable you to reflect upon the journey you have made in your professional development. Many experienced teachers find keeping a reflective journal a useful source of professional development, a decade or more after they qualified.

CONCLUSION

Your development as a teacher is individual and unique because it builds upon the knowledge, understandings, skills, beliefs and values that you brought, and that brought you, to teaching in the first place. It is not, however, an isolated development. You will develop as a reflective practitioner through discussions with all those engaged in your course, fellow students, tutors, mentors, classroom assistants and other adults, and, indeed, the pupils in your schools. Those charged with overseeing your development, therefore, will want to see how you:

- respond to the feedback they receive from others;
- develop skills in sharing and discussing your own practice and that of colleagues;
- use self-review to identify specific ways of improving their practice; and
- set yourself learning goals and targets.

Your teaching cannot be based solely on producing quantifiable learning outcomes. As a teacher your role is not simply limited to the systematic transmission of knowledge in a school. If you concentrate on practical teaching skills and methods – the mechanics of teaching – it is possible that you might become a teacher who is able to manage a class and instruct pupils with a fair show of competence. However, as a reflective professional you will need to become aware of the larger social, economic and political context of their teaching. You will need to develop the flexibility to anticipate change and to adapt your methods to new challenges.

Ultimately, you will come to see your daily teaching in the perspective of larger theories of human development and social policy.

It is sometimes thought that reflective practice began in the 1980s. However, this belief is entirely erroneous as the following quotation from Benjamin Dumville's *Teaching: Its nature a varieties* shows. It was published seventy years ago:

> It is not usually the business of the individual teacher, least of all the young teacher, to decide absolutely what knowledge is of most worth ... But if he does not understand the principles upon which the selection of subjects is based, he can hardly be expected to carry out teaching in the proper spirit. If a teacher does not appreciate the general aims of education he will not fully appreciate the general aims of school education; if he does not appreciate the general aims of school education, he will not fully appreciate the aims of his special grade or any one special subject; if he does not have fairly clear ideas of the year's work as a whole or of what each subject as a whole ought to accomplish for the scholars, he will not know exactly what he is about in any particular day's work. The teacher is something more than the carpenter who follows without reflection the architect's plan ...
>
> (1933: 9–10)

Whilst we might wish to raise an issue concerning language and gender, Dumville's notion of reflective practice still has currency.

9 Professional Responsibilities

The last of the QTS Standards relating to Professional Values and Practice (1.8) requires that teachers '…are aware of, and work within, the statutory frameworks relating to teachers' responsibilities' (TTA, 2003). One way of approaching this is to start by learning what the statutory frameworks set out, and then to use this to work out what responsibilities are involved. New teachers, though, face multiple responsibilities from their first day in school, and there is an immediate need to get to grips with what exercising professional responsibility means in real everyday situations. We have therefore chosen to approach this Standard by concentrating on real situations reported by student teachers, identifying the specific responsibilities each situation involves, and discussing these responsibilities against the background of both statutory and non-statutory frameworks.

It should be noted that this chapter is *not* a comprehensive guide to the 'law for teachers'. It is primarily concerned with examining the nature of professional responsibilities as a central feature of teachers' work in schools. It is not confined to responsibilities located only within *statutory* frameworks, and starts by widening the field to explore both statutory and *non-statutory* frameworks as the contexts which determine teachers' responsibilities. What is non-statutory can be just as important as what is statutory in this respect. The chapter offers a way of conceptualising the *multi-dimensionality* of teachers' professional responsibilities. As we shall see, most situations teachers encounter require the simultaneous exercising of responsibilities in different areas, and managing this by balancing different kinds of responsibilities against each other is an essential professional skill. We present several examples of actual situations faced by student teachers which are typical of situations or experiences you may well face yourself. We invite you to become actively involved in considering questions about them. Supporting commentaries elaborate the multiple dimensions of responsibility implied by each situation, and references to relevant features of both statutory and non-statutory frameworks are provided for more detailed follow-up. We turn first to what is meant by statutory and non-statutory frameworks.

THE 'STATUTORY' AND THE 'NON-STATUTORY'

'Statutory' means: of or pertaining to statute, that is, 'a written law passed by a properly constituted authority, e.g. an Act of Parliament' (Nelson Contemporary English Dictionary). The strictly statutory frameworks are:

- Legislation: Acts of Parliament;
- 'Orders' issued by the Secretary of State for Education under powers granted by legislation;
- GTCE Professional Code of Practice, backed by legislation; and
- Contracts of Employment: subject to the general law of such contracts.

Legislation passed by Parliament includes Acts which are not exclusively confined to Education. Very importantly, it includes general legislation such as the Disability Discrimination Act 1995 or the 1976 Race Relations Act and its Amendment in 2000. The latter imposed a new general duty on public authorities 'to make the promotion of race equality central to all their functions' (Document Summary Service, 2002). Both the 'Orders' issued by the Secretary of State for Education and the GTCE's *Code of Professional Values and Practice for Teachers* (GTCE, 2002) have statutory status with the force of 'enabling' Acts of Parliament behind them. The GTCE has powers conferred by legislation which include granting and removing an individual teacher's licence to teach in maintained schools in England. 'Orders' are issued which cover many detailed aspects of education policy. Since the 1988 Education Reform Act, which gave the Secretary of State extensive powers in this respect, the English education system has been increasingly directed and regulated through such Orders, often in the form of DfES 'Circulars'. The most important set of principles governing teachers' statutory responsibilities and working time is contained in the School Teachers' Pay and Conditions Act, which is supported by an annual *Teachers' Pay and Conditions of Service* document. Teachers' individual contracts of employment set out, usually in detailed job specifications, the particular responsibilities attached to their appointments, and are subject to general contract and employment law. As a result of government policy (DfES, 2003) a wide range of day-to-day routine responsibilities formerly carried out by teachers is being passed to support staff. Some of the most important are: chasing absences, producing standard letters, collating pupil reports, administering and invigilating examinations, ordering supplies and equipment, minuting meetings and collecting money.

Teachers' professional responsibilities are framed by all of these statutory instruments, but they are also framed by other factors which have varying kinds of status, including *non*-statutory status. Among the most important non-statutory frameworks are:

- Headteachers' discretionary authority;
- 'Guidance' issued by various statutory bodies;
- School policies; and
- Professional custom and practice.

The status of headteachers' authority is an interesting case. Headteachers of *maintained* schools (but not, it should be noted, those of *independent* schools) are bound by the national pay and conditions regulations, but the discretionary authority which they have is considerable, and can be instrumental in determining teachers' specific responsibilities. Teachers' job descriptions, for example, typically include clauses like, 'and such other duties and responsibilities as the headteacher may require'. Insofar as a job description is usually an adjunct to a contract of employment, this kind of clause has statutory status supported by employment law.

Moving to the domain of what is more clearly non-statutory, the most important is 'Guidance' issued by the DfES, OFSTED, or other agencies such as the TTA. But even the status of this can be somewhat uncertain. DfES guidance documents are usually marked, 'Status: Recommended', but at least one document on inclusive schooling is called, somewhat oddly, 'Statutory Guidance'. In practice, 'Guidance' contains recommendations which can often have substantial influence on schools, and on individual teachers' work. Most of the National Strategy policy, for example, is driven by non-statutory 'Guidance', and the operational detail of school inspections also resides in handbooks of guidance issued by OFSTED. Few schools, however, ever regard OFSTED guidance as in any sense 'optional'!

Another class of instruments which have a significant bearing on teachers' professional responsibilities is the interesting example of school policies. Schools are statutorily required to have formal institutional policies on many aspects of their governance and internal arrangements. Formally speaking, these are *written*; and they are 'passed' by a *properly constituted body* – the Governing Body of a school – which itself has formal legal standing supported by parliamentary acts. By virtue of this, and the fact that most policy statements are responses to statutory regulations, they have considerable 'legal' force. However, such formal policy statements are entirely dependent on how the policies they describe or define are actually put into practice, which leaves considerable scope for marked variations both between schools and even within an individual school for 'operational slippage'. In secondary schools, for example, responsibility for certain things is devolved to subject departments or year divisions. An example might be a school's policy for marking pupils' work. Much depends on the consistency with which that kind of policy is managed in different departments. Finally, there is the whole issue of professional expectations which derive from custom and practice: unwritten; not, normally, the product of systematic formulation; but, nevertheless, powerful determinants of professional responsibilities, protocols and conduct generally.

In some ways, it is this last area of uncodified professional practice which is the most important of all to consider, precisely because it represents a body of professional knowledge and a tradition of practice which is largely undocumented and implicit, and therefore more difficult for new professionals to 'access' compared with written codes, the law and teacher certification requirements. It is also the area in which ethical and moral issues often emerge in ways that can be problematic simply because of the absence of an explicit code of practice. It is vital to 'tune into' this implicit professional culture accurately and promptly. It informs many aspects of professional life within an individual organisation, and plays a particularly important part in defining professional expectations and responsibilities at an institutional level. The features of this culture are what you might expect to be reflected if you were to ask the question, 'What is it really like to work in this school?' It is the kind of question you might well ask teachers you meet when visiting a school for a job interview.

It is because both statutory and non-statutory frameworks inform teachers' professional responsibilities that this chapter takes a broad view and is not limited to statutory frameworks. We will see later in a number of authentic situations how both kinds of frameworks intersect in reality and make demands on how teachers make decisions and respond appropriately to challenging or problematic circumstances.

PROFESSIONAL RESPONSIBILITY – FOR WHAT, AND TO WHOM?

The concept of responsibility involves notions of holding some sort of charge or trust for a task, service or office invested in you, and accountability or liability for its discharge to others. Hence, we generally talk about being responsible *'for* something, *to* somebody'. The situation is immediately multi-dimensional in *professional* responsibilities because there are several potential 'others' to whom, in different situations, responsibility may be due. For teachers, the dimensions of responsibility can be listed as follows:

- SELF: to oneself;
- COLLEAGUES: to colleagues in the immediate environment of the school;
- PROFESSION: to the teaching profession in general;
- CHILDREN: to children and their parents or carers;
- SCHOOL: to the school as an institution within a particular community; and
- SOCIETY: to society as a whole.

Particular dimensions may have primacy in any given situation, but in practice many of the six dimensions are usually 'in play' most of the time. It is very difficult, for example, to separate responsibility to immediate colleagues from responsibility to the school as an institution, and therefore from responsibility to society as a whole. As a preliminary exercise, consider this first authentic situation arising from a student teacher's school experience:

Situation 1 During one lunch time I observed a group of pupils smoking behind the science block. What should I have done/said?

Try ranking all six dimensions above in order of their importance in this situation. To whom is a teacher in this situation *primarily* responsible? You are allowed to 'fudge' things by according some dimensions equal standing, but – to force you into making some hard decisions – you must place just one of the six dimensions first on its own, and only one of them last on its own.

Here is a rather different situation. Again, rank the six responsibility dimensions for this situation following the same rules, and compare the outcome with Situation 1.

Situation 2 On an afternoon off I saw a pupil out of school on his own during school hours. He saw me see him, but I did not know whether to ignore him, greet him, or tell him off. Since I was not sure and I was not a permanent teacher at the school I said hello and walked on.

Which dimensions are most and least in play when you compare them? For which dimensions did you have most difficulty deciding an importance ranking? Was that difficulty different in the two situations?

Let us take Situation 2 a bit further by asking not just 'To whom is a teacher primarily responsible?' here, but also, 'What are they responsible *for?*'

School attendance/truancy is obviously the issue, but how far is it part of a *teacher's* professional responsibilities to take action on this in the circumstances described?

Now work through these questions:

1   Is the fact that the student teacher is not a 'permanent teacher at the school' significant? The student clearly thinks so, but do you agree?
2   What are teachers' responsibilities (if any) regarding the conduct of pupils out of school?
3   Does the matter of school hours have any bearing on the whole matter?

Before leaving the issue of school attendance, it is worth noting that under certain circumstances – for instance, truancy cases taken to court – school registers can be presented as evidence. This applies as much to teachers' records of attendance in individual lessons as it does to tutor or class group registrations for morning or afternoon school sessions. The implications of this are clear, especially for teachers in secondary schools where classes move from lesson to lesson under different teachers between the main twice-daily registrations: you are responsible for checking and recording attendance in every lesson.

Even in these first two relatively 'simple' examples, then, we can begin to see quite tricky questions arising concerning *what* teachers are professionally responsible for, and *to whom*. The demands such situations make on their knowledge of 'the law' – at whatever level of statutory formality – can be challenging and complex.

One more question before moving too far away from Situation 1: Why might the age of the pupils have possible legal implications within the school's wider local community?

REALMS OF PROFESSIONAL RESPONSIBILITY

We will return to more examples like these, but it is necessary to step back from the detail of particular situations for a moment in order to 'map' the main realms in which teachers typically have professional responsibilities. The best way to do this is with a visual tool like a 'mind map' (Buzan and Buzan, 2003). The one that follows places 'Responsibilities' at the centre, and adopts the six 'responsibility dimensions' identified earlier as its main lines or branches. The representation here does not take every branch out to its thinnest twig, although some have been extended quite a long way for illustrative purposes .

No claims are made about the sophistication of this particular mind map's representation of teachers' responsibilities. Far from it; it is no more than a tentative attempt. It is interesting, for example, that the curriculum, teaching, learning and the whole range of responsibilities teachers have for decisions about methods, resources, activities, the sequencing of topics, managing the classroom, assessment and so on – their pedagogical responsibilities – arose associatively from the 'Society' line out of 'Education System'. Another mind mapper might well see it very differently.

There are three reasons for representing professional responsibilities in this way. First, it breaks down a highly complex subject into easily identifiable components. Second, it enables us to see more clearly the relationships between the frameworks and contexts which define work in schools and the responsibilities teachers have within them. To this end, some elements of those frameworks are appropriately positioned around the periphery of the mind map to direct your attention to connections between key features of the statutory and non-statutory landscape of education and particular kinds of responsibility. Third, you may find it interesting to generate your own more complete mind map for the topic. It would be an excellent way of building your own conceptualisation of teachers' professional responsibilities, and a worthwhile introduction to this kind of powerful and adaptable brain 'tool' if you have not explored it before. If this is the case, do prepare yourself by reading the book by the Buzan brothers.

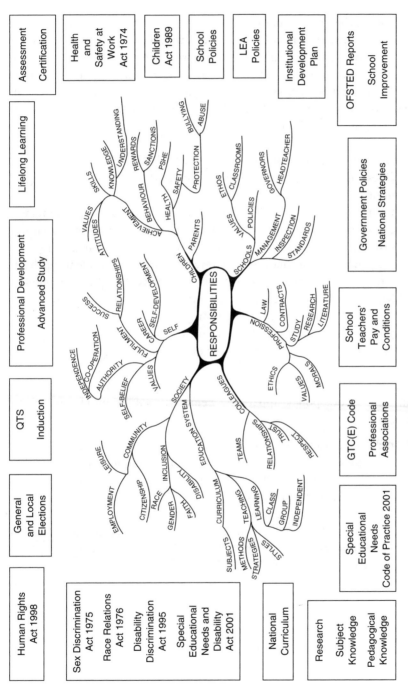

Human Rights
Act 1998

General
and Local
Elections

QTS

Induction

Professional Development

Advanced Study

Lifelong Learning

Assessment

Certification

Sex Discrimination
Act 1975

Race Relations
Act 1976

Disability
Discrimination
Act 1995

Special
Educational
Needs and
Disability
Act 2001

Health
and
Safety at
Work
Act 1974

Children
Act 1989

School
Policies

LEA
Policies

Institutional
Development
Plan

OFSTED Reports

School
Improvement

National
Curriculum

Research

Subject
Knowledge

Pedagogical
Knowledge

Special
Educational
Needs
Code of Practice 2001

GTC(E) Code

Professional
Associations

School
Teachers'
Pay and
Conditions

Government Policies

National Strategies

RESPONSIBILITY DIMENSIONS

RESPONSIBILITY IN ACTION: REAL SITUATIONS

This section of the chapter presents five more authentic situations encountered during school experience by student teachers on a PGCE course. The situations do not necessarily fit *neatly* into one of the six main 'dimensions' of the mind map. Most of them involve responsibilities in more than one dimension. Their principal map locations are suggested, but you may have your own ideas about other locations which are equally (or more) important in each situation.

The format of what follows for each situation is:

1   Situation: presented in the student teacher's own words;
2   Questions: to answer on your own or in discussion with colleagues or tutors and mentors;
3   Commentary: discussing each situation, highlighting dilemmas and considering possible responses to the questions. You may want to postpone reading a commentary until you have thought or talked through the situation and the questions. To avoid confusion, student teachers are referred to as 'teachers', and school students as 'children' or 'pupils';
4   Map Locations: suggestions about where the situation in question lies on the map of responsibility dimensions; and
5   References: to relevant legislation and other regulatory requirements including, where appropriate, key quotations from guidance.

We start with a situation which raises questions about a teacher's responsibilities in relation to a school policy apparently being ignored by pupils and staff colleagues alike.

Situation 3   There is a school policy of no running in the corridors, but few children pay any attention to it. When I confront pupils I am ignored. I think that not many of the staff pick up on this which is why there is such disrespect for this policy.

I would like to be able to fall back on some form of discipline, but as this usually involves a detention, to which these children do not necessarily turn up, and it all becomes so time consuming because you must chase them up, do you ignore the running?

Questions

1   Do you 'go with the flow' and ignore the running?
2   What can one teacher do on his or her own to implement a neglected school policy?
3   Whose responsibility is it to re-activate the policy and make it effective?
4   Does it really matter?

Commentary

Policies which are not consistently implemented command no respect. There are big issues here. One is health and safety, and the school could be in trouble for negligence if a pupil or an adult were injured. Another is the failure of senior management, in which it would seem someone is not taking seriously their responsibility for 'driving' the policy. The conscientiously minded teacher who wants to do something about it has his or her own authority undermined, and being ignored in the corridor is quite likely to make that authority harder to establish in the classroom. Other things follow for this teacher: diminished respect for professional colleagues; lower levels of self-actualisation and higher stress. Yes, of course it matters: for this teacher; for other teachers; for the pupils and their parents; for the school and its image as an orderly place or otherwise in the community.

Map locations Children...Safety, Parents, Care; School...Policies, Management; Colleagues...Respect, Teamwork; Self...Authority, Fulfilment.

References

Children Act 1989.
Health and Safety at Work Act 1974.
The school's health and safety policy.
The school's behaviour and discipline policy.

> 'Teachers have a statutory duty to do all that is reasonable to protect the health, safety and welfare of pupils. This statutory duty of care is reinforced by the terms of their contract of employment and by their pastoral responsibility towards pupils – which entails recognising that children have a fundamental right to be protected from harm' (Document Summary Service, 2002: 9).

Situation 4 Very personal remarks made about my clothing: 'Nice jacket, Miss. Do you have a shirt that goes with it? I prefer your other suit', etc. Where do I draw the line? Obviously designed to provoke.

Questions

1   How would you respond to such comments?
2   What professional responsibilities are involved here?

3   Is it possible that the teacher might be wrong about the comments being 'obviously' designed to provoke?

4   How can she exploit this situation constructively in terms of developing a positive relationship with this class?

Commentary

This is a good example of the boundaries between the 'personal' and the 'professional' being challenged (as discussed in Chapter 6), but on this occasion by pupils rather than colleagues. Question 4 is well worth thinking about carefully. The way the teacher responds is critical for how her relationship with the pupil develops in future. If she jumps down the pupil's throat, she risks reinforcing any tendency the pupil may have for disaffection. This raises an important point about professional responsibility generally. It is all too easy to react impulsively in highly pressurised working conditions. Time to think is a luxury that mostly occurs after the event. A strong and *actively working* sense of responsibility – or multiple responsibilities, reflecting obligations in the different realms of responsibility we have mapped – is a safeguard against impetuosity and the risk of responding inappropriately. It holds together all those values, beliefs and dispositions which are part of your professional 'persona' and inform the way you act, and the way others see and respond to you in your professional roles.

There are two main issues in Situation 4: how the teacher reacts at the personal level, defending her own privacy and maintaining appropriately respectful behaviour; and the impact her response has on the pupil concerned. The teacher might be sensible to pass the remark off lightly and not to bridle at it, aiming to maintain a positive rapport with the pupil and avoid confrontation which could easily alienate the pupil. Perhaps a quiet word in private with the pupil to encourage her to be less personal, outspoken or provocative? Some may feel, however, that this is taking inclusion too far, and not doing enough to 'draw the line' and establish the limits distinguishing acceptable from unacceptable behaviour. There is plenty to debate here.

Map locations   Self...Self-belief, Relationships, Success; Children...Behaviour; Profession...Values; Society...Inclusion.

References

DfEE Circular 10/99: Social Inclusion: Pupil Support.
Evaluating Educational Inclusion: Guidance for Inspectors and Schools (OFSTED, 2000).

Situation 5 A pupil on a class outing to the churchyard round the corner was walking over the gravestones and others thought it was impressively daring. I told him to stop (I wasn't the class teacher) as it was disrespectful, and as he didn't, and I didn't want to walk onto the graves myself, I yanked him back. (In the lab, also, I can see that sometimes physical restraint may have to be used for safety reasons.)

Questions

1   Was the teacher right to 'yank him back'?
2   What are the risks?
3   In what circumstances are teachers legally permitted to use physical force to restrain pupils?

Commentary

This is a highly problematic issue. As you might expect, the law is detailed and complex. It is also, at critical points, less than decisive. A section of the 1996 Education Act (Section 550A) makes it clear that in non-extreme circumstances (defined as, for example, self-defence from attack or an immediate risk of injury) teachers 'may use such force as is reasonable in all the circumstances'. But 'there is no legal definition of *reasonable force*' (Document Summary Service, 2002: 42). Among the circumstances in which physical restraint might be deemed reasonable are when it is to prevent a pupil from causing damage to property, or from 'engaging in behaviour prejudicial to maintaining good order and discipline at the school' (which includes authorised *out-of-school* activity, as in this situation).

Situation 5 is about physical restraint. But what about physical contact with pupils generally? It is *not* the case that any physical contact with a child is in some way unlawful. DfES guidance on physical contact with pupils (DfES Circular 10/95, paragraph 49) makes clear that:

> 'It is unnecessary and unrealistic to suggest that teachers should touch pupils only in emergencies. Particularly with younger pupils, touching them is inevitable and can give welcome reassurance to the child. However, teachers must bear in mind that even perfectly innocent actions can sometimes be misconstrued. Children may find being touched uncomfortable or distressing for a variety of reasons. It is important for teachers to be sensitive to a child's reaction to physical contact and to act appropriately. It is also important not to touch pupils, however casually, in ways or on parts of the body that might be considered indecent.'

Teachers have a critical responsibility to be extremely cautious about any form of physical contact with pupils, and to be absolutely certain that any contact is appropriate not only to the situation but also in its manner.

The whole issue is fraught with risk and demands the highest levels of professional responsibility. That includes the absolute imperative for teachers to familiarise themselves with, and act according to, both the statutory requirements of the law and the non-statutory guidance produced by several government departments: the DfES, the Department of Health and the Home Office.

As described by the student teacher, the situation falls right on the borderline of what might be accepted as justifying physical restraint. The case *against* the use of force is principally that no one is in physical danger (as in fighting). However, it could be argued that the pupil is 'engaging in behaviour prejudicial to maintaining good order and discipline', and *could* be about to cause damage to property. It might also be seen as the out-of-school equivalent of 'seriously disrupting a lesson' and persistently refusing to obey an order from the teacher. Any of these *might* justify physical intervention, so long as the force applied is '*reasonable*' and 'in proportion to the circumstances of the incident'. On the other hand, the 'circumstances of the incident' might be regarded as insufficiently serious to justify physical restraint. We would need to know more than the brief description tells us, including exactly what 'yanked him back' amounted to. Apart from the bravado which appears to be diverting other pupils from the purposes of the visit, and the pupil's refusal to respond to a verbal instruction, the teacher sees the misdemeanour as, essentially, a moral one (note the word 'disrespectful' in the description). It is very difficult to anticipate what weight this would carry if there had been a formal complaint against the teacher and an investigation. This takes us on to the second question, 'What are the risks?' There are two main risks. The first is that the pupil might react violently to the contact and attack the teacher physically, in which case the whole situation escalates gruesomely. The second is the possibility of a complaint being made against the teacher by the pupil's parents. This has to be taken as a serious possibility in any instance of physical contact with pupils by teachers, as we know only too well from a number of headline cases. In this specific case, and in all cases where force is used, the teacher's first immediate professional responsibility is to 'report the matter orally to the headteacher or a senior member of staff, and provide a written report as soon as possible afterwards'. That is more than a 'recommended' course of action. It is essential action in any such incidents.

Finally, it is worth noting in relation to corporal punishment that, 'It continues to be unlawful for a teacher to use any degree of physical contact which is deliberately intended to punish, or to cause pain, injury or humiliation...regardless of the seriousness of the behaviour or the degree of provocation' (Document Summary Service, 2002: 42).

Map locations   Children...Behaviour, Safety, Parents, Abuse; Profession ...Law, Morals, Ethics; Self...Career.

References

The Children Act 1989.
DfEE Circular 10/95: Protecting Children from Abuse.
Education Act 1996, Section 550A: The Use of Force to Control or Restrain Pupils.
'Whatever the situation, teachers should always be aware that whenever they touch a child their actions may be misconstrued' (Document Summary Service, 2002: 18).

All of the situations so far have centred on incidents arising from pupil behaviour and teachers' responses to it. Each one of them, though, has involved thinking about responsibilities in several different areas of our 'map'. The multi-faceted nature of what may appear to be a fairly straightforward and clear-cut issue is characteristic of virtually every situation you are likely to encounter, and it is what makes decisions about how to respond a serious matter. This is all the more the case for new teachers encountering complex situations in professional life for the first time. The absence of 'experience' means that there is little or no personally accumulated knowledge of similar or equivalent situations from the past to inform decisions about how to respond. What experience provides as it grows over time is an increasingly rich and sophisticated 'memory' in which the kinds of incidents or problems we have been looking at are situated, ready for recall as precedents to help in handling a new problem. Moreover, that memory interconnects discrete and different past situations, diffusing each one's distinctiveness, so that relationships and patterns build up and become very powerful mental structures 'organising' the intelligence we bring to bear on decisions about action. The 'lessons' learned from every discrete experience are all available as each new experience is encountered.

To some extent this happens automatically. It is part of the way memory works. But there is no doubt that it can be assisted by processes of deliberate reflection and analysis – of applying ourselves to identifying patterns and relationships and consciously searching for and making connections: 'discovering our mind's favourite movements in approaching events, in making manageable shapes out of experience' (Hoggart, 1971). Hoggart's way of putting it – and particularly that word 'favourite' – emphasises the personal and subjective forces at work, which is natural since his context is the language we use and the ways we connect with other people. In the context of professional responsibility, and particularly in considering how professional responsibility is located within certain formally established frameworks of legal, moral, occupational and professional expectations, what becomes necessary for the individual professional is 'squaring' their own 'favourite movements in approaching events' with those 'external' established frameworks which regulate the conditions in which professionals work. This is, in many ways, the ultimate professional responsibility: finding satisfactory accommodations between personally preferred ('favourite') ways of doing things and what is acceptable to and endorsed by the professional environment. We can illustrate this by another authentic situation which reveals a pronounced clash between the teacher's preferred way of handling chatty pupils and the formal school policy – where that accommodation between 'personally preferred' and 'institutionally acceptable' is yet to be found.

Situation 6 ASSERTIVE DISCIPLINE

Procedure for chatting pupils:

1st warning

2nd warning: moved in class

3rd warning: sent out of class

This leads to children often being sent out of the classroom. I have grave misgivings about this. If you try not to send children out you end up being inconsistent:

(a) within the school policy; and

(b) within a single class.

Victims of this policy are sometimes children who are chatty but not at all malicious, and are repentant when you tell them the error of their ways. I don't want some children excluded from my lessons.

Questions

1   What is, in your view, this teacher's 'preferred' way of handling chatty pupils?

2   In what ways does this preferred strategy actually clash with the school policy?

3   What would you suggest the teacher should do to achieve a satisfactory accommodation between the two?

4   Would the teacher be acting irresponsibly by ignoring the clash and pursuing their own preferred strategy in the interests of maximising inclusion?

Commentary

Situations like this occur all the time in schools, where individual teachers' own particular ways of doing things – often demonstrably successful and effective, and developed over many years – are in tension with some aspect of formally established policy. The key question is, 'What are the limits to personal autonomy, where responsibility to institutional norms takes precedence over responsibility to personal professional values and beliefs?' It is, as it happens, an extremely topical issue in education as successive governments have made the regulatory frameworks stronger and wider in scope. Teachers are having to review autonomous personal practice which has become 'intuitive' in the light of new policy requirements and priorities. Finding ways of accommodating what have become intensely valued and long-held professional principles within new required strategies and approaches is not always at all straightforward.

It was noted earlier that there can be marked variations in how a policy is implemented even within a single school, and in Situation 6 you have the example of this difficulty made real in one teacher's practice. It is complicated by the fact that it is not just a personal preference that is at stake for this teacher. Their personal preference is legitimised by being based firmly on a strong sense of responsibility to promote inclusive practices. This in turn is high on the official educational agenda, and supported by both statutory and non-statutory instruments. What you have here, then, is a dilemma confronting an individual teacher: 'My way, or the school's way?'; and a dilemma confronting the school: 'This version of assertive discipline, or something else which does not compromise inclusion?' In fact, this teacher, as a PGCE student on school experience, may well be ahead of the school in prioritising inclusion. At the moment, though, it looks as if the teacher is caught in 'Catch-22': on the one hand, implementing the assertive discipline policy and thereby keeping faith with responsibilities to the school and other staff means irresponsibly compromising inclusion principles; and on the other, responsibly pursuing the inclusion principles means declaring irresponsible unilateral independence from an agreed school policy. An interesting little problem for the school management system, and perhaps the way forward is for the teacher concerned here to see it in that way, and to take steps to raise it at that level.

Map locations   Society . . . Inclusion; Schools . . . Policies, Management; Self . . . Values.

References

The Human Rights Act 1998.
DfEE Circular 10/99: Social Inclusion: Pupil Support.
'An unambiguous whole-school policy should enable teachers to establish a clear framework for their own classroom discipline. They should set up rules and routines which are linked to the school's high expectations of good behaviour

and to its sanctions for behaviour which is unacceptable' (Document Summary Service, 2002: 40).

Situation 6 is an example of where 'personal' and 'institutional' professional responsibilities collide, but where both have legitimate foundations in well-established and declared policies and principles. We can extend this, though, to situations where policies and principles are much less declared and explicit, and are the emanations of what was called at the beginning of the chapter 'custom and practice' – the unwritten and not systematically formulated (or even declared) expectations that influence professional conduct. One of the areas in which this sometimes arises for new teachers, and particularly those who are training on college and university courses and may still see themselves as 'students', is that of personal presentation when going into schools. 'Personal presentation' is a somewhat euphemistic term for 'what you look like', and covers dress, hairstyle and, these days, jewellery, especially visible piercings. Without being prudish about it, it also needs to include tattoos and personal hygiene. There are no statutory frameworks establishing what teachers' responsibilities are in this area – just custom and practice – and what is acceptable varies from school to school.

Such are the sensitivities involved with some of these highly personal matters that, as a famous advertisement for a breath deodorant once put it, 'Even your best friends won't tell you'. Well, let this book at least give it to you straight. Rightly or wrongly, all these things matter, and are part of every teacher's professional responsibilities. Teaching involves close proximity to children, and if you smell they will know it, and may well exploit it. Take personal responsibility for ensuring that this kind of issue never arises. It is as simple as that. Dress is not so simple, because fashions change and schools vary greatly, but in this, as with every aspect of personal appearance, it is crucial to recognise that how you appear to pupils is part of your 'implicit communication' with them, sending out important signals. If the school rule for pupils is 'No nose studs', you can hardly fulfil a responsibility to play your part in applying it if you are wearing one. It is going to sound very peremptory and even old-fashioned, but if you find yourself seriously at odds with the professional norms of an institution you are in, you have two choices: change or leave. That is not to say that certain reasonable things are not worth working to change. In the late 1960s and early 1970s, for example, female teachers successfully battled against the resistance of some schools to recognise trouser suits as acceptable professional dress. It was not confined to schools; the same battle went on in businesses and factories. It was not unassociated with the then current fashion for mini skirts, whose impracticality for teachers in classrooms could become all too obvious. Things do change, but custom and practice can be quite trenchant.

Our final situation takes us into the very important field of professional responsibility for child protection.

Situation 7 What do you do if a Year 9 pupil comes up to you after registration at 2.30 pm on a Friday in tears because he/she claims he/she is a victim of physical and emotional bullying?

The alleged culprits are older pupils, and the 'victim' insists that he/she wants no action taken on his/her behalf. You were due 5 minutes ago to teach 31 Year 7 pupils.

Questions

1   What *do* you do?
2   What should you *not* do?
3   What should be your response to the pupil's insistence that 'no action' is taken on his or her behalf?

Commentary

The situation is an example of disclosure of abuse being suffered by the pupil, and raises all the responsibilities under the Children Act 1989 for teachers to do all that they can to protect children from harm. Bullying is one of the most common forms of abuse, and emotional, or 'verbal', bullying is as serious as physical bullying. It is worth noting that over half of primary (51%) and secondary school pupils (54%) thought that bullying was 'a big problem' or 'quite a problem' in their school, and that just over half (51%) of pupils in Year 5 reported that they had been bullied during the term, compared with just over a quarter (28%) in Year 8 (DfES Research Report, 2003). It would be quite wrong to regard a disclosure about bullying in school as any less serious than other forms and locations of child abuse. Very, very sadly, we know that bullying in school can have tragic consequences. All schools are now required to have a specific policy on bullying.

As you consider your responses to Question 1, there are several things you should be thinking about. First, the welfare of the child is paramount. The fact that the teacher is already late for their next lesson is something that needs to be managed within this priority. It is therefore worth considering what steps are possible for the teacher in this respect. Second, the timing of the pupil's disclosure could be very significant. This also merits consideration. Third, it is essential to be aware that under Sections 27 and 47 of the Children Act, LEAs and schools have a statutory duty 'to assist local authority social services departments when they are acting on behalf of children in need or enquiring into allegations of child abuse' (Document Summary Service, 2002). This includes 'a pastoral responsibility for protecting children from harm', and having in place a child protection policy with which all teachers are familiar. All schools have a 'designated teacher' (usually at deputy head level in secondary schools) 'who is responsible for receiving information about cases of suspected abuse'. Because no one can predict when a child may make a disclosure, this is one area of the law and the school's policy that all teachers *must* be familiar with *before* they face the experience of disclosure. Fourth, a key responsibility of the teacher receiving the disclosure is to pass on information to the designated teacher. It could be, and our example situation may well be in this category, that there is real urgency about doing this: Friday afternoon; a journey home imminent; a weekend ahead. Teachers must also 'make a written note of any discussion held with the child and pass this on to the designated teacher. This note should record the date, time, place, the people who were present and what was said.'

As you consider Question 2, you must be aware that your 'chief task at this stage is to listen', taking care not to ask 'leading questions' or impose your own assumptions. It might be helpful to rehearse this in role-play with a colleague in order to examine exactly what this calls for if you face this responsibility. This is important because what passes between a disclosing child and the person they disclose to 'can affect the evidence in any subsequent criminal proceedings'.

Question 3 raises the critical issue of confidentiality. Whatever your personal inclinations, your *professional obligation* is to avoid promising confidentiality to a disclosing child. It is your responsibility to share disclosed information within appropriate professional contexts:

> if a child confides in a teacher and requests that the information is kept
> secret, s/he must tell the child sensitively of this responsibility,
> and not give any guarantee of absolute confidentiality. Nevertheless,
> the child should be assured that the matter will only be disclosed to
> those who need to know, and that any such disclosure is for the child's
> own sake.
>
> (Document Summary Service, 2002: 17)

Here too, it is worth rehearsing with a colleague the ways you might do this. Finding the right words for the very first time under highly pressurised circumstances, as in Situation 7, is very difficult indeed.

The limits of individual teachers' involvement in child protection matters are tight and precise:

> It is important for teachers to remember that they are *not* responsible for
> investigating cases of suspected abuse – this is the role of the local
> authority social services departments (SSD), the police and the NSPCC.
> Nor must they take any action beyond that set out in the procedures
> established by the local Area Child Protection Committee (ACPC) and
> incorporated into the school's protection policy. For the classroom

teacher, the main procedure is to pass on information to the designated teacher and then to co-operate, as required, with the school, the LEA, the SSD and other agencies.

(Document Summary Service, 2002: 16)

Child protection procedures are designed to maximise inter-agency collaboration, in which the designated teacher is the school's link representative. It is possible that in a case of bullying, the school will first seek to deal with it internally in accordance with its formal policy before referring it to other agencies, and most cases of bullying within school are successfully handled in this way. This is not, though, a decision that is within the responsibility of an individual teacher receiving a specific disclosure, or becoming aware through observation that a pupil is being bullied. It *must* be referred to the designated teacher for them to determine what action to take.

Map locations   Children... Protection, Safety, Bullying.

References

The Children Act 1989.
DfEE Circular 10/95: Protecting Children from Abuse.
DfES/Department of Health 1999: Working Together to Safeguard Children: a Guide to Inter-agency Working to Safeguard and Promote the Welfare of Children.
DfES Guidance 0064/2000: Bullying – Don't Suffer in Silence (Revised September 2002).
OFSTED Report (HMI 465, March 2003): Bullying: Effective Action in Secondary Schools.
DfES Research Report (RR400, May 2003): Tackling Bullying: Listening to the Views of Children and Young People.

CONCLUSION

This chapter has concentrated on looking in some detail at the complex nature of teachers' professional responsibilities. The complexity stems from the fact that in any given situation it is almost always the case that a number of dimensions of responsibility need to be considered. It is quite possible that this could involve interests which conflict with each other. At the very least, decisions about how to respond or proceed require a well-developed capacity for mental 'parallel processing' of distinct considerations, recognising that a particular issue involves, for example, a mixture of self-interest, obligations to children or staff colleagues, expectations deriving from your membership of a professional community and legal imperatives.

Developing that capacity for 'parallel processing' is a career-long enterprise. It has at least four phases. The first phase, in initial teacher education and training, is one in which you are discovering responsibilities and each new situation tends to loom large as a discrete set of circumstances to be managed 'for the time being'. It can be challenging because at this stage you are very much in the process of building an individual 'professional persona' in which a huge array of values, personal attitudes, skills and knowledge begins to cohere as 'experience'. This phase is characterised by a strong sense of responsibility to self and a concern to demonstrate personal competence and success, especially within the contexts of professional certification for QTS and its ratification during the induction period.

The second phase is characterised by a gradual shift towards a stronger sense of wider responsibilities within the structures of professional work and life: working collaboratively with colleagues; seeing one's professional responsibilities as part of a bigger picture in terms of pupils' development, the work of other staff and the school as a whole, and, importantly, in terms of personal professional development. Patterns of understanding about your own place in the broader context contribute to bringing discrete professional values and knowledge into greater coherence as a personal value system. Connections and relationships shape experience and provide greater confidence in managing specific responsibilities.

The centrality of personal professional development in this second phase brings us back to the 'map' of 'responsibility dimensions'. Some of the features on the periphery of the map are rather different from the statutory and non-statutory frameworks with which we have been mainly concerned. The picture of professional responsibilities would be seriously incomplete if these features were not included. They include: professional development and advanced study; research, subject knowledge and pedagogical knowledge; professional associations and lifelong learning. A reference to general and local elections is also included as a way of suggesting the active interest teaching professionals should take in the politics of education. Teachers have responsibility for 'maintaining and developing their skills, knowledge and expertise', and keeping up to date with 'new findings, ideas and technologies' (GTCE, 2002). This kind of responsibility need not be – indeed, *should* not be – limited to keeping in touch with what others are doing; becoming involved in research and developmental initiatives is also a professional responsibility.

The third phase is one where that confidence in taking responsibility becomes an ambition or interest in and for itself, reflected, for example, in readiness to accept a significant role in some aspect of institutional activities: co-ordinating a team; chairing a working party; heading a department; taking an active role in mentoring new teachers and so on. A strong sense of 'responsibility to self' still continues, but the shift in this phase is towards interests in creating and sustaining some of the structures and frameworks which support other individual colleagues in the actualisation of their responsibilities.

The fourth phase is represented in schools by movement towards positions of overall responsibility: headships and deputy headships characterised by leadership responsibility for all of the structures and frameworks which support the school as a whole community.

A quick sketch like this runs risks of terrible over-simplification. In particular, there is the danger that it is taken as defining a *desirable* ladder of career progression. This is emphatically *not* the intention. Perhaps the greatest professional responsibility of all is that of recognising clearly and honestly the kinds of responsibility you are equipped to take, and reaching decisions about personal career development which give that self-knowledge all due weight. It is, however, a reminder that the notion of professional responsibility is not something fixed and static. Just as Chapter 1 explored aspects of how being a professional teacher develops over time, so we end this chapter by noting that professional responsibilities themselves shift over time according to personal position and interests within the profession.

NOTES

Full details of official documents cited are provided in the Reference sections in Part 4 of this chapter.

Further useful references are provided in *The Bristol Guide* and in Annex A of *Qualifying to teach: Handbook of guidance* (TTA, 2003).

Afterword

We referred in the Introduction to the importance of 'joining things together in practice', and in Chapter 8 to 'the process of synthesising'. Having looked at each of the QTS Standards for Professional Values and Practice separately, we end by returning to this. Mature professionalism involves being able to bring together knowledge, understanding and experience from many different domains. Our ambition must be to work towards holding together, in our daily practice, around some central personal values the kinds of things with which this book has been concerned. It is a demanding personal challenge.

Teaching is a highly complex business. It combines much that is routine with a very great deal that is non-routine, calling for the exercise of professional judgement time after time every day, often in tricky and pressured situations. Dealing with what is routine – or appears to be routine – is helped by reference to previous experience of similar situations. Our responses in such cases tend to acquire something of the status of precepts or rules through habit or regular rehearsal. Dealing with the non-routine – the unexpected, the problematic, the new and unfamiliar, the paradoxical – is never straightforward precisely because of the absence of close specific parallels on which to base responses. While experience can point us in certain directions, there must always be improvisation and risk-taking in such situations.

It is at such moments that professional judgement is most tested, and heavily dependent on the existence of value and ethical systems which direct us towards making sound decisions. Professional judgement is at its most fragile and insecure at such moments, especially for beginning teachers whose professional value and belief 'systems' are more likely to be emergent than established. We should be cautious, however, about people who present themselves as fully 'established' or certain in their practice and values: that way may lie dogmatism and complacency. The quest for security in personal values is fuelled by reflection, and reflection is also the prophylactic against complacency and professional stagnation. That is why such importance attaches to reflection, and why the goal of being a 'reflective practitioner' is so currently pervasive in professional discourse and underpins everything in this book.

Being a reflective practitioner, though, is not unproblematic, as Chapter 8 explored in some detail. There are different things to be reflective *about*; reflection can take different *forms*; and it can operate at different *levels*. Evaluating a lesson, for example, may be something done privately, or assisted by an observing mentor. It could be concerned with the specific strengths and weaknesses of a lesson with a view to making immediately actioned adjustments or establishing longer-term targets. It might take the form of written notes, or a conversation. It might involve consideration of entirely personal and individual practice, or broader issues such as school policies. It might be your own teaching that you are reflecting on, or someone else's. It can be as much concerned with philosophies of education as with particular technical teaching matters.

The natural tendency for beginning teachers to be most concerned with technical features of their personal teaching practice has been noted. At a deeper level, however, is the need to *reflect on the activity of reflection itself*, in which the practice of reflection itself becomes the subject of scrutiny and development. This is just as important in the process of being a reflective practitioner as deliberately engaging learners in 'learning about learning' is to the learning process. The more knowledgeable learners are about the processes of learning they are engaged in, the more effective will their learning become. Similarly, the more deliberate you are in considering the processes of reflection you are engaged in, the more effective will this feature of your developing professionalism become. It is through reflection at deeper levels that we refine those personal and professional value systems which help us to handle non-routine and problematic situations which do not lend themselves to simple technical solutions.

We would press this even further by proposing that now more than ever we need teachers who are prepared to engage in questioning and refining their own personal and professional values and, from this position, to assert their voices and practice in the educational system. Part of this involves being prepared to take risks and to experiment, and to question orthodoxies of policy and practice, from whatever sources they emanate. These orthodoxies have become increasingly powerful and institutionalised in the English educational system since the late 1980s, and we need to ensure that doors to alternative ideas are kept open. Every teacher has a part to play in this, but their authority and legitimacy in contributing to debate about practice and policy depends on their readiness to examine their own practice and professional value and belief systems analytically and responsibly.

This cannot be pursued without looking outside one's own practice, and outside the prevailing orthodoxies and paradigms which inform that practice, to new ideas, methods, techniques and principles. It includes looking at both theory and practice. Theory is not, as it has sometimes been pejoratively characterised, something that exists separately from practice. It arises from developments in practice, through efforts to conceptualise and organise understandings that emerge from practice. Conversely, new kinds of practice take life from efforts to implement theoretical perspectives. There is growing acceptance of this in the increasing emphasis being placed on teaching as a research-based profession. Being a 'reflective practitioner' involves, essentially, researching your own practice. But we need to understand this in two ways: using your own practice as the site of your own research; and using the research into practice elsewhere to expand your vision of possibilities and to authenticate your own ideas.

Where does this leave us?

First, as new teachers facing the requirements of QTS, you need, of course, to accumulate *evidence* of your successful engagement with and achievement of the Standards. The ways in which you do this will largely be determined by the procedures, arrangements and methods of documentation in place in the particular initial teacher education programme you are pursuing. We hope that the questions and tasks we have posed have augmented the resources available to you for this.

Second, you should approach the Standards in the first section of *Qualifying to Teach* concerned with Professional Values and Practice with as much *application* as you extend to those in the other sections. As the individual chapters of this book demonstrate, there is as much to think about, to explore in practice and to research further in these eight Standards as there is in others which may appear to be more closely related to technical aspects of your practical teaching.

Finally, you should look *beyond* the specific ways in which the Professional Values and Practice Standards are formulated and worded in *Qualifying to Teach*. As they stand, these formulations are but pointers towards some of the most central and fundamental features of teachers' professional activity and behaviour. We have been concerned in this book not only to support your practical achievement of what these Standards explicitly set out and expect, but also to encourage you to go beyond them, and to engage intellectually with some of the research and professional literature on these important issues.

In about 1877 (the date is not precisely recorded), a textbook for teachers was published written by a certain Henry Kiddle and others: *How to teach: a graded course of instruction and manual of methods for the use of teachers*. One cannot help feeling that while the media of publication have developed, and the Internet has become a prime source of such guidance, little else has changed and there is still a major industry in the publication of material 'for the use of teachers', including, of course, the book before you. Indeed, the Internet seems to have spawned quite a cascade of courses of instruction and manuals of methods. We might do well to reflect on one bit of wisdom that a book from well over a century ago contains, though:

> teachers are constantly to be reminded that habits are always more
> valuable than facts – that it is not the quantity of knowledge acquired
> that constitutes a criterion of mental advancement, but the mode of

> employing the mental faculties – the *habits of thought* into which the
> mind has settled in making its acquisitions or in applying them.

What matters most are the habits of thought into which your mind settles as
you discriminate between all that is on offer to guide and support your teaching.
We trust that thinking about values and the moral and ethical dimensions of
teachers' work will be a constant habit of your own professional thought.

Bibliography

Abraham, J. (1993) *Divide and School: Gender and Class Dynamics in Comprehensive Education*, London: Falmer Press

Archard, D. (1993) *Children: Rights and Childhood*, London: Routledge

Arthur, J. (2003) *Education with Character: The Moral Economy of Schooling*, London: RoutledgeFalmer

Arthur, J., Davison, J. and Moss, J. (1997) *Subject Mentoring in the Secondary School*, London: Routledge

Ashworth, P.D. and Saxton, J. (1990) 'On Competence', *Journal of Further and Higher Education*, 14 (2), 15–27

Avis, J. (1994) 'Teacher Professionalism: One More Time', *Educational Review*, 46 (1), 63–72

Ball, S. (1981) *Beachside Comprehensive: A Case Study of Secondary Schooling*, London: Cambridge University Press

Balshaw, M. and Farrell, P. (2002) *Teaching Assistants: Practical Strategies for Effective Classroom Support*, London: David Fulton Publishers

Bercik, J.T. (1991) 'Teacher Education and Development of Proactive/Reflective Pre Service Program', *Education*, 112 (Winter), 200–205

Berliner, D. (1994) 'Teacher Expertise', in Moon, B. and Shelton Mayer, A. (eds) *Teaching and Learning in the Secondary School*, London: Routledge

Bhatia, V. (1995) *Analysing Genre: Language Use in Professional Settings*, London: Longman

Bloom, B.S. (ed.) (1956) *Taxonomy of Educational Objectives: The Classification of Educational Goals. Handbook 1, Cognitive Domain*, New York: McKay

Bloom, B.S., Hastings, J.T. and Madaus, G.F. (1971) *Handbook on Formative and Summative Evaluation of Learning*, New York: McGraw-Hill

Blum, A.L. (1990) 'Vocation, Friendship and Community: Limitations of the Personal-Impersonal Framework', in Flannagan, O. and Rorty, A.O. (eds) *Identity, Character and Morality: Essays in Moral Psychology*, Cambridge MA: MIT Press

Bolton, E. (1994) 'The Quality and Training of Teachers', in *Insights into Education and Training*, Paul Hamlyn Foundation, National Commission on Education, London: Heinemann

Bonnett, M. (1996) 'New Era Values and the Teacher–Pupil Relationship as a Form of the Poetic', *British Journal of Educational Studies*, 44 (1), 27–41

Bourdieu, P. (1973) *Outline of a Theory of Practice*, Cambridge: Cambridge University Press

Bowles, S. and Gintis, H. (1976) *Schooling in Capitalist America: Education and the Contradictions of Economic Life*, London: Routledge & Kegan Paul

Bridges, D. and Kerry, T. (eds) (1993) *Developing Teachers Professionally: Reflections for Initial and In-service Trainers*, London: Routledge

Broadfoot, P. (1989) *Reports to Parents on Student Achievement: The UK Experience*, University of Bristol, Working Paper No. 2/89 October

Brown, R. (ed.) (1973) *Knowledge, Education and Cultural Change*, London: Javistock

Brown, G. and Wragg, E.C. (1993) *Questioning*, London: Routledge

Burstyn, J. (1980) *Victorian Education and the Ideal of Womanhood*, London: Croom Helm

Buzan, T. (with Buzan, B.) (2003) *The Mind Map Book*, Revised edition, London: BBC Publications

Calderhead, J. (ed.) (1987) *Exploring Teachers' Thinking*, London: Cassell

Calderhead, J. (1989) *Teacher's Professional Learning*, London: Falmer

Campbell, E. (2000) 'Professional Ethics in Teaching: Towards the Development of a Code of Practice', *Cambridge Journal of Education*, 30 (2), 203–21

Capel, S., Leask, M. and Turner, T. (2003) *Learning to Teach in the Secondary School: A Companion to School Experience*, (3rd edition), London: Routledge Falmer

Carr, D. (1993a) 'Guidelines for Teacher Training: The Competency Model', *Scottish Educational Review*, 25 (1), 17–25

Carr, D. (1993b) 'Moral Values and the Teacher: Beyond the Pastoral and the Permissive', *Journal of Philosophy of Education*, 27 (2), 193–227

Carr, D. (1993c) 'Questions of Competence', *British Journal of Educational Studies*, 41 (3), 253–271

Carr, D. (2000) *Professional Values*, London: Routledge

Carr, D. (2003) *Making Sense of Education: An Introduction to the Philosophy and Theory of Education and Teaching*, London: Routledge

Carr, W. and Kemmis, S. (1986) *Becoming Critical. Education, Knowledge and Action Research*, Lewes: Falmer

Central Office of Information (COI) (1975) *Women in Britain*, London: HMSO

Centre for Studies on Inclusive Education (CSIE) (2000) *Index for Inclusion: Developing Learning and Participation in Schools*, Bristol: CSIE

Chappell, C. and Hager, P. (1994) 'Values and Competency Standards', *Journal of Further and Higher Education*, 18 (3), 12–23

Chrispeels, J. (1996) Effective Schools and Home-School Partnership Roles: A Framework for Parental Involvement, *School Effectiveness and School Improvement*, Vol. 7, pp. 297–323

Claxton, G. (1999) *Wise Up: The Challenge of Lifelong Learning*, London: Bloomsbury

Coldron, J. and Smith, R. (1999) 'Teachers' Construction of their Professional Identities', *Journal of Curriculum Studies*, 31 (6), 711–726

Cole, K. (2002) *The Complete Idiot's Guide to Clear Communication*, Cambridge: Alpha Books (Pearson Education)

Cole, M. (ed.) (2002) *Professional Values for Teachers and Student Teachers*, London: RoutledgeFalmer

Davison, J. (1998) 'Your Pastoral Role' in Capel, S., Leask, M., and Turner, T. *Starting to Teaching the Secondary School*, London: Routledge

Davison, J. (2000) 'Literacy and Social Class' in Davison, J. and Moss, J. *Issues in English Teaching*, London: Routledge

Davison, J. and Dowson, J. (2003) *Learning to Teach English in the Secondary School 2nd Edition*, London: Routledge

DES (1975) *Education Survey 21 – Curricular differences for boys and girls*, London: HMSO

DES (1987) *The Report of the Task Group on Assessment and Testing (TGAT)*, London: HMSO

DES (1992) *Initial Teacher Training (Secondary Phase)* (Circular 9/92), London: DES

Dewey, John (1933) *How We Think: A Restatement of the Relation of Reflective Thinking to the Educative Process*, London: D.C. Heath

DfEE (1998) *Teachers: Meeting the Challenge of Change*, London: HMSO

DfEE (1999) Report of the National Advisory Group on PSHE, *Preparing Young People for Adult Life*, London: HMSO

DfES (1998) *Requirements for Courses of Initial Teacher Training; Teaching: High Status, High Standards* (Circular 4/98), London: HMSO

DfES (2000) *Working with Teaching Assistants – A Good Practice Guide*, London: HMSO

DfES (2002a) *Schoolteacher's Pay and Conditions Document* (The 'Blue Book'), London: HMSO

DfES (2002b) *Time for Standards: Reforming the School Workforce*, London: HMSO

DfES (2003) *Raising Standards and Tackling Workload: A National Agreement*, London: HMSO

DfES/TTA (2002) *Standards for the Award of Qualified Teacher Status*, London: HMSO

Dillon, J. and Maguire, M. (2001) *Becoming a Teacher* (2nd edition), Buckingham: Open University Press

Document Summary Service (2002) *The Bristol Guide: Teachers' Legal Liabilities and Responsibilities*, Bristol: University of Bristol Graduate School of Education

Douglas, J. (1964) *The Home and the School*, London: MacGibbon and Kee

Downie, R.S. (1990) 'Profession and Professionalism', *Journal of Philosophy of Education*, 25 (2), 147–159

Dumville, B. (1933) *Teaching: Its Nature a Varieties*, London: University Tutorial Press

Elbaz, F. (1992) 'Hope, Attentiveness and Caring for Differences: The Moral Voice of Teaching and Teacher Education', *Teaching and Teacher Education*, 25 (2), 147–159

ELLI (2003) www.beinglearnercentred.co.uk

Elliott, J. (1989) 'Teacher Evaluation and Teaching as a Moral Science' in Holly, M.L. and McLouglin, C.S. (eds) *Perspectives on Teacher Professional Development*, London: Falmer Press

Eraut, M. (1994) *Developing Knowledge and Competences*, London: Falmer Press

Everard, B. (1995) 'Values as Central to Competent Professional Practice', in Busher, H. and Saran, R. (eds) *Managing Teachers as Professionals in Schools*, London: Kogan Page

Farrell, P., Balshaw, M. and Polat, F. (2000) *The Management, Role and Training of Learning Support Assistants*, London: DfEE (DfEE Research Report 161)

Fisher, R. and Ury, W. (1999) *Getting to Yes: Negotiating an Agreement Without Giving In* (2nd edition), London: Random House Business Books

Floud, J., Halsey, A. and Martin, F. (1966) *Social Class and Educational Opportunity*, Bath: Chivers

Friedman, A. and Phillips, M. (2003) Codes of Conduct in the Professions: Do they meet the challenge? *Real World, Real People: Conference Proceedings*, 2–4 September 2003, University of Surrey Roehampton, London

Frost, D. (1993) 'Reflective Mentoring and the New Partnership' in McIntyre, D. (ed.) *Mentoring*, London: Kogan Page

Furlong, J. and Maynard, T. (1995) *Mentoring Student Teachers: The Growth of Professional Knowledge*, London: Routledge

Furlong, J., Barton, L., Miles, S., Whiting, C. and Whitty, G. (2000) *Teacher Education in Transition*, Buckingham: Open University Press

Gaskell, J. (1985) 'Course Enrolment in High School: The Perspective of Working Class Females', *Sociology of Education*, 58, pp. 48–59

General Teaching Council for England (2002) *Code of Professional Values and Practices for Teachers*, General Teaching Council for England: London

Gillborn, D. and Gipps, C. (1996) *Recent Research on the Achievements of Ethnic Minority Pupils*, London: OFSTED

Gillborn, D. and Mirza, H.S. (2000) *Educational Opportunity*, London: OFSTED

Goldstrom, J.M. (1972) *Elementary Education 1780–1900*, London: David & Charles

Goodlad, J. (1990) *Teachers for Our Nations Schools*, San Francisco: Jossey-Boss

Griffiths, M. and Tann, S. (1992) 'Using reflective practice to link personal and public theories', *Journal of Education for Teaching*, 18, 69–84

Guirdham, M. (2002) *Interactive Behaviour at Work* (3rd edition), Harlow: Pearson Education

Habermas, J. (1974) *Theory and Practice*, London: Heinemann

Halsey, A.H., Floud, J. and Anderson, C.A. (eds) (1961) *Education, Economy and Society*, London: Collier-MacMillan

Halsey, A.H. (1998) 'Leagues Apart' in *The Times Higher Education Supplement*, 6

Halstead, M.J. and Taylor, M.J. (2000) 'Learning and Teaching about Values: A Review of Recent Research', *Cambridge Journal of Education*, 3 (2), 169–202

Hargreaves, A. (1994) *Changing Teachers, Changing Times: Teachers' Work and Culture in the Postmodern Age*, London: Cassell

Hargreaves, D. (1967) *Social Relations in the Secondary School*, London: Routledge & Kegan Paul

Hargreaves, D. (1982) *The Challenge for the Comprehensive School*, London: Routledge & Kegan Paul

Hay McBer (2000) *Research into Teacher Effectiveness: A Model of Teacher Effectiveness* (DfEE Research Report 216), London: DfEE

Haynes, F. (1998) *The Ethical School*, London: Routledge

Helsby, G. (1999) *Changing Teachers' Work*, Buckingham: Open University Press

Hoggart, R. (1971) *Only Connect: On Culture and Communication* (BBC Reith Lectures 1971), London: Chatto & Windus

Hoyle, E. (1995) 'Changing Conceptions of a Profession', in Busher, H. and Saran, R. (eds) *Managing Teachers as Professionals in Schools*, London: Kogan Page

Hoyle, E. and John, P.D. (1995) *Professional Knowledge and Professional Practice*, London: Cassell

Husen, T. and Postlethwiate, T.N. (eds) (1994) *The International Encyclopedia of Education* (2nd edition), Oxford: Pergamon

Hyams, O. (1997) What Does It Mean to be *in loco parentis?*, *Education and the Law*, Vol. 9, No. 3, pp. 187–194

Hyland, T. (1993) 'Professional Development and Competence-Based Education', *Educational Studies*, 19 (1), 123–132

Hyland, T. (1996) 'Professional, Ethics and Work-Based Learning', *British Journal of Educational Studies*, 44 (2), 168–180

Jalongo, M. and Isenberg, J. (1995) *Teachers' Stories: From Personal Narrative to Professional Insight*, San Francisco: Jossey-Bass

Kamm, J. (1971) *Indicative Past: A Hundred Years of the Girl's Public Day School Trust*, London: Allen & Unwin

Kelly, A.V. (1995) *Education and Democracy: Principles and Practices*, London: Paul Chapman

Korthagen, F.A. and Wubbels, T. (1995) 'Characteristics of Reflective Practitioners: Towards an Operationalization of the Concept of Reflection', *Teachers and Teaching: Theory and Practice*, 1 (1), 51–73

Krathwohl, D.R., Bloom, B.S. and Masia, B.B. (1964) *Taxonomy of Educational Objectives: The Classification of Educational Goals. Handbook 2, Affective Domain*, New York: McKay

Lacey, C. (1970) *Hightown Grammar*, Manchester: Manchester University Press

Lawton, D. (1973) *Social Change, Educational Theory and Curriculum Planning*, London: University of London Press

Lee, B. and Mawson, C. (1998) *Survey of Classroom Assistants*, NFER/Unison

Maguire, M. and Dillon, J. (2001) *Becoming a Teacher: Issues in Secondary Teaching*, Buckingham: Open University Press

McCombs, B.L. (2002) *How Can We Define Teacher Quality? The Learner-Centered Framework*, Paper presented at the American Educational Research Association annual meeting, New Orleans, April 2002

McGettrick, B. (2002) *Unpublished Conference Paper, University of Bristol, November 2002*

McIntyre, A. (1981) *After Virtue*, Notre Dame: Notre Dame Press

McIntyre, A. (1985) *After Virtue* (2nd edition), London: Duckworth

McIntyre, A. (1995) 'The Idea of an Educated Public', in *Education and Values: The Richard Peters Lectures*, London: Institute of Education

McIntyre, D. (ed.) (1993) *Mentoring*, London: Kogan Page

McLaughlin, T.H. (1994) 'Values Coherence and the School', *Cambridge Journal of Education*, 24 (3), 453–470

Mehrabian, A. (1981) *Silent Messages: Implicit Communication of Emotions and Attitudes*, Belmont: Ca., Wadsworth

Ministry of Education (1959) *Education of the Adolescent* (Crowther Report), London: HMSO

Ministry of Education (1963) *Half Our Future* (Newsom Report), London: HMSO

Musgrave, P.W. (1968) *Society and Education in England since 1800*, London: Methuen

National Board for Professional Teaching Standards (1989) *What Teachers should know and be able to do*, Arlington, VA, National Board for Professional Teaching Standards, www.nbpts.org/about/coreprops.cfm

National Curriculum Council (NCC) (1990a) Curriculum Guidance 7 *Environmental Education*, London: HMSO

National Curriculum Council (NCC) (1990b) Curriculum Guidance 8 *Education for Citizenship*, London: HMSO

Naylor, F. (1996) 'Need to Clear the Fog around Values', *Times Educational Supplement*, 5 July

Neville, S. (1993) 'Shared Values', in Selmes, C.S.G. and Robb, W.M. (eds) *Values and the Curriculum: Theory and Practice*, London: National Association of Values in Education and Training

Nias, J., Southworth, G. and Yeomans, R. (1989) *Staff Relationships in the Primary School*, London: Cassell

Neill, S. (1993) *Body Language for Competent Teachers*, London, Routledge

Nixon, J., Martin, J., McKeown, P. and Ranson, S. (1996) *Encouraging Learning: Towards a Theory of the Learning School*, Buckingham: Open University Press

Norris, N. (1991) 'The Trouble with Competence', *Cambridge Journal of Education*, 21 (3), 331–341

Oakley, J. and Cocking, D. (2001) *Virtue Ethics and Professional Roles*, Cambridge: Cambridge University Press

Office for Standards in Education (OFSTED) (1993) *The New Teacher in School*, London: HMSO

OFSTED (1999) *Raising the Attainment of Minority Ethnic Pupils: School and LEA Responses*, London: Central Office of Information

OFSTED (2000) *Evaluating Educational Inclusion: Guidance for Inspectors and Schools*, London: Stationery Office

OFSTED (2001) *Managing Support for the Attainment of Pupils from Minority Ethnic Groups*, London: Stationery Office

OFSTED (2003) *Framework for Inspection*, Ofsted: London

O'Hear, A. (1988) *Who Teaches the Teachers?* Research Report No. 10, London: The Social Affairs Unit

Organisation for Economic Cooperation and Development/Human Resources Development Canada (OECD) (1997) *Literacy Skills for the Knowledge Society: Further Results from the International Adult Literacy Survey*, Paris: OECD

Osborn, M., McNess, E. and Broadfoot, P. (2000) *What Teachers Do: Changing Policy and Practice in Primary Education*, London: Continuum

Peters, R.S. (1965) *Ethics and Education*, London: Allen & Unwin

Pring, R.A. (1992) 'Academic Respectability and Professional Relevance', Inaugural lecture delivered before the University of Oxford on 8 May 1991, Oxford: Clarendon Press

QCA (1998) *Report of the Advisory Group on Citizenship* (Crick Report), London: HMSO

QCA (1999a) *National Curriculum for England* (Key Stages 1 and 2), London: HMSO

QCA (1999b) *National Curriculum for England* (Key Stages 3 and 4), London: HMSO

Rudduck, J. (1991) *Innovation and Change*, Milton Keynes: Open University Press

Rutter, M., Maughan, B., Mortimer, P. and Outston, J. (1979) *Fifteen Thousand Hours: Secondary Schools and Their Effects on Children*, Wells: Open Books

Schön, D.A. (1983) *The Reflective Practitioner: How Professionals Think in Action*, New York: Basic Books

Scottish Office Education Department (SOED) (1993a) *Guidelines for Teacher Training Courses*, Edinburgh: SOED

Sharpe, S. (1976) *Just Like a Girl: How Girls Learn to be Women*, Harmondsworth: Penguin

Social Trends (1992) Central Statistical Office, Social Trends No. 22: 1992 edition, London: HMSO

Sockett, H. (1993) *The Moral Base for Teacher Professionalism*, New York: Teachers College Press

Soltis, J.F. (1986) Teaching Professional Ethics, *Journal of Teacher Education*, 37 (3), 2–4

Stationery Office (1999) *The Stephen Lawrence Inquiry: Report of an Inquiry/by Sir William Macpherson of Cluny; Advised by Tom Cook, The Right Reverend Dr John Sentamu, Dr Richard Stone; Presented to Parliament by the Secretary of State for the Home Department by Command of Her Majesty. February 1999*, London: Stationery Office

Strain, M. (1995) 'Teaching as a Profession: The Changing Legal and Social Context' in Busher, H. and Saran, R. (eds) *Managing Teachers as Professionals in Schools*, London: Kogan Page

Strike, K.A. (1995) 'The Moral Responsibilities of Educators' in Sikula, J. (ed.) *Handbook of Research on Teacher Education*, New York: Macmillan

Teacher Training Agency (TTA) (2000) *Raising the Attainment of Minority Ethnic Pupils: Guidance and Resources for Providers of Initial Teacher Training*, London: TTA

Teacher Training Agency (2004) *Questions: A CDROM Resource*, London: TTA/Education Broadcasting Trust

Tickle, L. (1996) 'Reflective Teaching: Embrace or Illusion?' in McBride, R. (ed.) *Teacher Education Policy: Some Issues Arising from Research and Practice*, London: Falmer Press

Tom, A.R. (1980) 'Teaching as a Moral Craft: A Metaphor for Teaching Teacher Education', *Curriculum Enquiry*, 10 (3), 317–323

Tomlinson, J. and Little, V. (2000) A Code of the Ethical Principles Underlying Teaching as a Professional Activity, in Garrdner, R., Cairns, J., and Lawton, D., *Education for Values: Morals, Ethics and Citizenship in Contemporary Teaching*, London: Kogan Page

TTA (2002 and 2003) *Qualifying to Teach: The Professional Standards for Qualified Teacher Status and Requirements for Initial Teacher Training*, London: DfES/HMSO

TTA (2003) *Handbook of Guidance*, London: TTA

Turner, B. (1974) *Equality for Some*, London: Ward Lock

Turner, A. and Turner, S. (1994) 'Multicultural Issues in Teacher Education in Science' in Thorp, S., Deshpande, P. and Edwards, C. (eds) *Race, Equality and Science Teaching: A Handbook for Teachers and Educators*, Hatfield: Association of Science Teachers.

Vygotsky, L.S. (1978) *Mind and Society: The Development of Higher Order Psychological Processes*, Cambridge: MA, Harvard University Press

Watson, B. and Ashton, E. (1995) *Education, Assumptions and Values*, London: David Fulton

Wentworth, W.M. (1980) *Context and Understanding: An Inquiry into Socialisation Theory*, New York: Elsevier

White, J. (1990) 'The Aims of Education', in Entwistle, N. (ed.) *Handbook of Educational Ideas and Practices*, London: Routledge

Whiting, C., Whitty, G., Furlong, J., Miles, S. and Barton, L. (1996) *Partnership in Initial Teacher Education*, London: University of London: Institute of Education

Whitty, G. and Willmott, E. (1991) 'Competence – based Approaches to Teacher Education Approaches and Issues', *Cambridge Journal of Education*, 21 (3), 309–318

Willis, P. (1977) *Learning to Labour: How Working Class Kids Get Working Class Jobs*, Sheffield: Saxon Press

Willis, P. (1981) 'Cultural Production is Different from Cultural Reproduction...', *Interchange*, 12 (2–3), 48–67

Wilson, J. (1993) *Reflection and Practice*, University of Western Ontario: Althouse Press

Index